Soft Words
FOR A HARD TECHNOLOGY

Soft Words
FOR A HARD
TECHNOLOGY

HUMANE COMPUTERIZATION

Brian R. Smith

A SPECTRUM BOOK

Prentice-Hall, Inc., Englewood Cliffs, New Jersey 07632

Library of Congress Cataloging in Publication Data

Smith, Brian R. (date)
    Soft words for a hard technology.

    "A Spectrum Book."
    Includes index.
    1. Electronic data processing—Psychological aspects.
2. Human engineering.   I. Title.
QA76.9.P75S63 1984   001.64   84-13297
ISBN 0-13-822438-2
ISBN 0-13-822420-X (pbk.)

10 9 8 7 6 5 4 3 2 1

ISBN 0-13-822438-2

ISBN 0-13-822420-X {PBK.}

Editorial/production supervision by Elizabeth Torjussen
Cover design © 1984 by Jeannette Jacobs
Manufacturing buyer: Pat Mahoney

Prentice-Hall International, Inc., *London*

Prentice-Hall of Australia Pty. Limited, *Sydney*

Prentice-Hall Canada Inc., *Toronto*

Prentice-Hall of India Private Limited, *New Delhi*

Prentice-Hall of Japan, Inc., *Tokyo*

Prentice-Hall of Southeast Asia Pte. Ltd., *Singapore*

Whitehall Books Limited, *Wellington, New Zealand*

Editora Prentice-Hall do Brasil Ltda., *Rio de Janeiro*

Contents

To Myrna M. Milani
    veterinarian
    author
    mother
    scientist
    philosopher

Acknowledgments

I wish to thank a number of people who, in one fashion or another, made this book possible:

Arthur P. Schwartz, literary agent, and Jim Gaughan, editor, who first gave me the idea.

Roger Sullivan, director of education at Commercial Union Automation Services, Inc., Boston, for insight on training and personnel requirements in the automated office.

John G. Kreifeldt, professor of design, Tufts University, for his help in some of the areas of software design.

Linda Pitkin, systems analyst at Boise Cascade's Paperboard Division in Brattleboro, Vermont, for her help (and that of her staff) with the use of friendly computer systems.

Myrna M. Milani, DVM, for all the careful editing and her own additions to the book that make it much more than what I had first intended.

Marjorie A. Zerbel, my intrepid typist and friend, for doing the entire manuscript—always on time and always perfect.

Sue A. Clifford, marketing manager, direct mail marketing of Uarco, Inc., of DeKalb, Illinois, for supplying me with the photographs of computer-related equipment. Readers who are interested in the furniture and related equipment offered by Uarco, as pictured herein, may call the firm toll-free at 800-435-0713.

John Grayson Kirk, executive editor at Prentice-Hall, Inc., who gave me the final go-ahead for the book itself.

The copy editors, graphics personnel, layout people, marketing folks, and others at Prentice-Hall who actually bring you this book.

Introduction

This is the Age of Information. As a technological society, we've placed information on a pinnacle consistent with our desire and ability to worship earthbound gods. If Alvin Toffler is correct, we've had three "ages" in our human development. In the first of these, we valued the ownership of land. Those who desired power controlled the land and all that came with it, which often meant the "ownership" of people themselves—fiefdoms, baronial holdings, slavery. The coming of the Industrial Revolution, especially in the United States, saw the end of slavery. We began, in a very small way, to lose our fascination with the accumulation of land as a means of demonstrating positions of power and looked toward the acquisition of capital—specifically, the ownership of assets (production facilities, machines, inventions)—as the basis of control. We revered individuals such as Rockefeller, Gould, Mellon, and Carnegie, who amassed capital and therefore controlled assets. They had the power. They were the new gods and held sway for about 100 years.

As a result of mathematical and engineering developments, in the middle 1940s we produced a machine capable of manipulating information. We were so fascinated with this wondrous device that we called it an electronic brain. The popular press of 1948 lauded the names of Vannevar Bush, Howard Aiken, J. Presper Eckert, and John Mauchly.

They were human beings who duplicated the human mind with telephone relays and common switches; or so they said.

Now almost forty years later, a device called an information processor brings us to the third stage of power—that belonging to those who control information. But unlike the Age of Land Ownership or the Age of Controlled Assets, this age is available to all. Information is cheap. IBM has shown that the cost of information processing, as measured by the expense to store or process one binary digit, has fallen well over a thousandfold in thirty years. We're now in an era in which anyone who chooses to have power (information) can do so with ease. Computers and computer terminals spring up on our desks, in our homes, and in our cars. Massive data bases of all kinds can be accessed with the stroke of a key.

As the computer, the word processor, and associated equipment multiply around the world, their impact is felt in nearly every part of our lives. We've become very clever in the manipulation of data, but this has not occurred without problems. Although we've designed these machines to operate at almost light speeds, few people—machine designers, engineers, office managers, or business owners—have given much thought to the human issues. Cathode ray tubes (CRTs) flash the instantaneous financial conditions of a business enterprise, but in many cases the human operator strains his or her vision at close range to observe a harsh depiction of green characters that, if used in the presence of fluorescent lighting, seem to blink at an unnatural frequency. Printers squeal with a sound equivalent to fingernails rasping down a blackboard. Terminals beep incessantly, sounding like a computer with hiccoughs. People leave their places of work with a new kind of fatigue, one caused by a new technology.

Thousands of workers consult their physicians with complaints of eyestrain, blurred vision, muscular ailments, and headaches. I suggest that some of these physical signs are as much a result of the human-human interaction, or in some cases the lack of it, as the human-machine factors. We can also use some of the information that we gain from ergonomics (literally, the measurement of work) to learn about the physical workplace and increase our knowledge of potential health hazards, however remote.

In the first chapter of this book, we discuss the physical and physiological elements connected with our computerized workplaces. There is more to say about humans and machines than just the discomfort that comes from a sore neck or a mild headache, although the causes of these conditions and their correction are addressed.

The second chapter deals with the interaction between human and computer, person and machine. It moves from the environment of the machine to the issues that face people dealing directly with the information process, the factors that affect their feelings and thoughts—in other words, their minds. We're not talking about the computer as something that can brainwash an operator or any other worker; but there are the issues of efficiency and productivity of "the automated worker." Much of Chapter 2 is devoted to those who deal more with software—systems analysts, programmers, operators, data processing and MIS managers—showing them the things that can be done to make administrative, professional, and managerial personnel feel more comfortable with the machine and what it can and cannot do. One of the most recent software innovations—interactive software—asks questions, poses possible solutions, and provides explanations through what is known as HELP routines; this is described in detail.

The subsequent chapters discuss the issues that affect the larger symbiotic relationship of human and machine. In Chapter 3, we'll look at the philosophy behind the fear of change. This chapter also serves as a transition into a study of the group effects of the information processor in the workplace. Chapter 4 is devoted to managers, supervisors, and executives, pointing out areas of concern both for them and for their people, as each affects the work environment. The final chapters focus on what we may call universal issues, with the last chapter discussing what's in store for us and computer technology in the years to come.

In my undergraduate days as a mechanical engineer in the late 1950s, I came across my first computer. It was an IBM 1620 that operated in a batch mode, meaning it only could work on one job at a time, one job after another. It only could be programmed in the FORTRAN language and used eighty-column punched cards to read both programs and data; it was agonizingly slow by today's standards and totally unforgiving (blanks had to be blanks and not zeroes). It couldn't even round numbers correctly (a calculated value of 4.0 would be shown as 3.99999). But, I had never been more fascinated with a machine in my life. After learning the elementary workings of this marvel and the rudiments of FORTRAN, I was in business. Now I had access to something that could extend my ability to compute. One of the first large-scale problems I tried was a multiple regression analysis of the various qualities of steel (density, hardness, ductility, shear strength) as a function of the amount and type of each alloying element—titanium, chromium, vanadium, nickel, and so on. I amazed myself with my newly discovered talents. As the 1960s and 1970s came and went, I saw what had started as a handful of computers drastically change and multiply. The electronic data processor is no longer either just a big, fast, accurate slide rule or a multimillion-dollar curiosity reserved for the elite. Direct progeny of the computer shrank size and cost but extended their capabilities in terms of memory size, basic processing time, language, and communications capabilities. They started to appear in shops and homes. Offshoots of the computer, such as the word processor, began appearing on peoples' desks. Finally, in 1982, *Time* magazine named the computer "The Machine of the Year." As I watched the computer change from something that once might well have taken a Ph.D. in mathematics as well as a master's in electrical engineering to understand and use to a machine that is now thought of as a home appliance, I also saw the effect that the technology was having on people. There are pluses and minuses. Here in the United States, entirely new companies and industries were born, providing jobs like those of programmer, computer design engineer, and systems analyst. Older methods gradually gave way to what was to be known as operations research.

On the negative side, many corporations, universities, nonprofit organizations, and government functions throughout the 1960s developed what Robert Townsend called computer priests: individuals who hid behind a plethora of terminology that very few could understand. Managers and executives became fearful that their data-processing folks would create such an intricate and incomprehensible hierarchy that eventually these interlopers would control the company and no one would know what they were doing. And what about electronic snooping? If you finance a new car or purchase an appliance on time, some computer somewhere will record that fact and, even with all our consumer protection legislation, that information could be recorded incorrectly.

There are many other issues that are the direct result of computers and information processing. The one that has been bothering many of us is the issue of the human being at his or her place of work. To be certain, the situation of efficient, safe, and pleasant working conditions is important, but more important is the human condition itself. We're now at the crossroads with electronic equipment, where careful, caring thought and concern must be given to the "people issue" or we may suffer some rather severe consequences. The two main concerns that I see are fear (along with its companion, ignorance) and loneliness or separation from other human contact.

In the late 1920s, the Western Electric Company in Cicero, Illinois, performed a now world-famous experiment. In an effort to discover whether lighting levels have an effect upon productivity, they selectively and gradually increased the illumination in the plant area. Productivity increased. Ergo, you make it brighter and people will work harder. Clear. Logical. Sensible. Now some genius wanted to see what would happen if lighting levels were decreased. "Well," the experts said, "people won't work as hard when it's dark. Any fool knows that, but if it'll make you happy, we'll try it." The maintenance staff began to put in lower wattage bulbs. At the height of this increasing darkness, the level of lighting in the manufacturing plant was equivalent to that of a full moon. And productivity increased again! Now the logic that was used before said: You make it darker and people will work harder. Not clear at all. Illogical. Nonsensible. Hardly, if you'll pardon the pun, enlightening.

To make a long study short, what the Hawthorne Study and later researchers discovered was that if you give workers attention, make them feel like human beings and not just a part of the production process, if you don't attempt to force them into a position in which they believe their free will is being violated, most of them will cooperate in helping to achieve overall organizational goals—whether that is a 15 percent return on net equity or simply higher quality typing with fewer mistakes. On top of everything else, they'll feel better about themselves. The point is that when people are dissatisfied with their work situation, it can often be traced to the fact that they are not getting enough attention. What device now stands as a potential hazard in the workplace to come between the needed interaction of human beings? You've got it. The work station of an information processor.

Let's run a brief scenario.

Jerry Stearns is a young, energetic, and bright person. He's twenty-five years old and a graduate of a business program at a large state university. When Jerry was interviewed by the Whirlwind Products Company, the people who eventually hired him spoke of an entry-level position in the sales department and an eventual move into a marketing analysis function. Jerry's good with numbers and has a flair for marketing.

Three years have gone by now. Jerry's a customer service representative (senior grade) at Whirlwind and hates his job. The work is dull, boring, and relatively routine. His boss rarely talks to him except on business matters, and then the communication is very formal. Jerry figures he'll be fired soon, but in a barroom conversation one Friday night with someone from the data-processing department, he learns a little bit more about the machine that sits at the end of his customer inquiry station. What he learns is enough to make him stay on at Whirlwind, at least for a while.

For several weeks, Jerry's a changed man at work. He comes in early and stays late: a model employee at Whirlwind, where they often judge extra hours as indicative of loyalty and therefore promotability. Jerry spends much more time at his terminal, which further pleases his boss. The boss figures Jerry's bringing himself more up to date on the status of customer orders. Actually, Jerry's learning two things that have nothing to do with the status of customer anything. Item 1: Jerry's learning to program. He got the rudiments of interactive COBOL from a textbook and is learning how to access data within company files. Item 2, and far more serious: Jerry is learning the security codes, some triple-level and constantly changing, of the data-processing system at Whirlwind. The latter comes from his systems-analyst friend who likes Jerry, Scotch, computers, and Whirlwind, in that order.

After about a month of "highly recommendable" behavior, Jerry slumps back into his old routine. He's sick on an occasional Monday or Friday, late three days out of five. Lackadaisical. Uninterested. Jerry starts arguing with the customers and, in one instance, calls the purchasing director of Whirlwind's largest customer "a . . . ing airhead," and that's it. Jerry's boss fires him, and gives him a month's severance pay, a handshake, and a wan smile. Jerry takes the next month to do a resumé, see a career counselor, and begin a mail-and-visitation job search with employers who might be interested in someone with marketing and data-processing experience. He has the severance pay, he has some money in mutual funds, and he can collect unemployment—which he does for about four weeks until he takes his present job at Hinsdale Research as a marketing analyst consultant specializing in marketing information systems.

Three days after Jerry takes his new job, Helen Raines, the data-processing operations manager (first shift), fires up the IBM System/380, Model 132. She knows there are some print runs left over from second-shift operations and that she had to load the three master files of Whirlwind: month-end financial data, marketing and sales report system, and production/quality information update. As she sets the printer to run from the output at logical disk drive 01, she loads the three other disks on drives 02, 03, and 04. She puts the master integrating program on drive 05 and fails to notice that a certain sequence of lights are illuminated on the 380's console that have never been lighted in that fashion before. If she had taken notice, what she would have seen would have alerted her to the fact that she should never have loaded the program file and typed "RUN" on the central console.

What happened next is literally anyone's guess. From the way that Helen tells the story, the program began to erase the master files of finance, marketing, and production. Billions of binary values were swept away with each electromagnetic impulse and in each microsecond—depending on the file that was being assaulted—one full year of accounting records were lost or three months' worth of all sales information on all customers worldwide were erased, or four weeks of the most intricate labor and production rates disappeared. While Helen oversaw a finicky 1400 line-per-minute printer, the 380 took every piece of information that was magnetically stored about the life and times of Whirlwind Products Company and altered its state to zero! Access codes were easily penetrated. The program's self-checks were overridden and then replaced with console messages like

WORKING

and

NO PARITY ERRORS ON LOGICAL UNITS 02-05

Once the data was destroyed, the program began to work on itself, erasing selected portions of its own instructions. Its nearly one million lines of code contained in subroutines tied to interconnecting functions linked to ancient programs like the payroll routine first written in 1961 were reduced piece by piece like ice masses falling from an iceberg. Finally, one statement was printed on the console as the machine halted:

GOOD-BYE

J. STEARNS

The master files and master programs were then no more. Helen did not keep backups of these ever-changing files, and Jerry knew that. Whirlwind, as a company, collapsed. Some of its divisions were picked up by large conglomerates for about ten cents on the dollar of net worth. Over 50 percent of the divisions totally lost their viability as business enterprises. About 6500 people lost their jobs. The company has tried to recover, but it, like so many other organizations, literally depended on its data-processing operation for survival. Fiction? Fantasy? Impossible? Not at all. It certainly could happen. What did our friend Jerry Stearns do? He wrote a small program that was hooked to the main operating program which compared the date that the computer was being operated with a certain preset date. If today's date was greater than this selected date, the program would operate normally, but if today's date were equal to or less than the preset date, the self-destruct routine was elicited. What was the preset date? It was thirty days after Jerry's last pay period, a day that was easily found by checking the payroll program.

We've all read about dissatisfied employees. When people are dissatisfied in a workplace, that feeling usually comes as a result of (1) not being appreciated, (2) not being told what's going on, and (3) not receiving attention. At least, those are the "big three" needs of American workers according to most surveys. When dissatisfaction sets in, some action usually occurs. It starts small: absenteeism, tardiness, turnover. It can grow to include insubordination, employee theft, even sabotage and violence. It's one thing for a disgruntled auto worker serving his or her piece of the production line to tie a fork inside the door of a Seville or put a dead hamster in the heater of an Omni. Look at the parallel that's already beginning to happen in our offices and work areas with computer terminals. People stick their faces into a CRT for the better part of a day with little human contact; and in many cases they must do what the computer tells them to or they'll be fired. How can you get back at that cold, unfeeling, impersonal machine? One solution is to do what Jerry did.

To be sure, there will always be Jerrys regardless of the environment, the supervision, the overall conditions of the job. I believe, though, that the issues of fear and loneliness can be faced without great disruption in an organization with computerized equipment; and once they are recognized and handled, people will feel better about the technology and about themselves as well.

I'll also propose some solutions to those problems that have come as a part of our electronic era, our Age of Information. I don't have *all* the answers though; some of them will come from you and your own desire to see things change. That's why there's something in this book for everyone who's a part of computer-related technology—from the small business owner about to install her first $15,000 data processor to the designers of hardware and software systems to the chief executive officer of a *Fortune 500* corporation.

We'll begin with some discussion of the physical workplace itself and then move rather quickly into the human issues. I urge all readers to think through carefully what I am saying here, for it could well change how many of you do business—whatever that business may be.

Physical and Physiological Factors

1

Ergonomics

We're hearing many new words in our computerized workplaces today, and one of those words is *ergonomics*. Quite literally, it means the measurement of work, but in a more simple and practical way it may be thought of as human factors engineering. Ergonomics combines human anatomy, psychology, physiology, and equipment design. The focus on human design factors for computer equipment has unfortunately come long after the emphasis on the technology of computer systems themselves. If humans are uncomfortable, or if they develop physical ailments as a result of working with computers, video display terminals (VDTs), or word processors, their productivity will decline and they won't be satisfied with the conditions of their jobs.

Sally Hanes has been working with her new word processor for about six months when she decides to visit her physician. She complains about blurred vision, headaches, and a general feeling of being out of sorts while at work. Sally's symptoms are not new to her doctor. He's listened to those same kinds of complaints from a number of men and women who work closely with VDTs. In all cases, he can prescribe a headache remedy or even tranquilizers, but he realizes that drugs or something like new eyeglasses don't get to the actual causes behind this degree of discomfort. His prescription to his patients is to change their physical workplace and their work routine (more breaks) or, if that can't be done, to change jobs.

Is computer equipment hazardous to our health? Should the Surgeon General require that warnings be posted on VDTs and keyboards? I don't think we've created dangerous conditions in our automated offices and production facilities, but there are several human factors that office managers, business owners, executives, and workers themselves should consider.

To be sure, almost every job can produce some form of physical discomfort. Computer terminals do seem to produce their own brand of ailments and, if we begin by recognizing the validity of these problems, we can all work to solve them.

I'm not only talking about physical discomfort and health problems. If equipment isn't designed with people in mind, the potential for error increases. Human adaptability, while great, can't always compensate for poor equipment design. A part of the 1979 disaster at Three Mile Island was attributed to the design and placement of both indicators and controls. Errors cost money. Errors waste time. Severe errors can cripple the efficiency of an organization.

There are simple things that can be done to lessen discomfort and fatigue. However, there's another element that is just as important as the design of the physical work environment: involvement. How many managers thrust computerized equipment on their subordinates without ever conferring with these same people? What's your attitude about something that's given you to do—something you had no part in creating? You don't feel very committed to it, do you? You'll probably complete the task, but there won't be much of a sense of ownership in it, and little enjoyment.

In 1982, Verbatim Corporation of Sunnyvale, California, surveyed 1263 office workers. Here is a summary of the results:

1. The fear that daily exposure to computer equipment will cause health problems is experienced by 68.2 percent of these office workers.
2. Eyestrain is a complaint of 63.4 percent of the people.
3. Nearly 80 percent believe better lighting is needed around VDTs.
4. More breaks, especially to rest their eyes, are desired by 78 percent.

Those statistics reflect the physical nature of work with computers. These workers were polled on other factors, and the survey also revealed that 87.3 percent of the office workers canvassed feel they should be allowed to participate in the selection of computer systems for the workplace and 78 percent want the right to attend vendor presentations before the company purchases a system.

The moral of this survey, and indeed the moral from the workplace itself, is this: Involve people who will be working with computers in the basic selection process. Listen to what they say regarding what they like and don't like. The people surveyed by Verbatim Corporation were mirroring what many workers experience today: a feeling of being left out, being cut off from what's happening, in addition to feeling physically uncomfortable with the computing equipment.

Physical Equipment

Once the typewriter was introduced into the office, it wasn't long before office furniture was designed to use it more effectively; secretaries and typists had special desks and chairs. Many pieces of computer equipment, however, are simply placed on desk tops or tables that were designed for other purposes.

If you're now in the process of selecting computer equipment, or if you have such equipment presently installed, give thought to the human factors and to human beings as well as to the software or the hardware.

One major concern about terminals relates to the keyboard. Most operators of VDT work stations will say that keyboards that are permanently attached to the VDT or CRT (cathode ray tube) or "screen," as it is sometimes called, aren't as easy to use as keyboards connected to the VDT with a flexible cable. Compugraphic Corporation of Burlington, Massachusetts, a manufacturer of computerized typesetting equipment, discovered that one of its European distributors was having the keyboards cut from the cabinetry and refinished as a unit separate from the video display. European operators found the separate keyboard to be more comfortable because it gave each person an opportunity to choose his or her own working position. As a result, Compugraphic changed its design.

Look at Figure 1-1 for a moment. Even though this table has been especially designed for computers, the arrangement with the detached keyboard in Figure 1-2 is more comfortable for the operator.

Let's briefly look at other enhancements to the modern workplace. Figures 1-3 and 1-4 are photos of other commercially available equipment. Figure 1-5 deserves special attention; notice that the screen may be swiveled and tilted to accommodate different operators or by the same operator to shift position. Also note that the keyboard can be tilted on its own stand, and an inclined footrest is provided for the operator.

Office furniture manufacturers and distributors responding to needs for greater comfort in the automated office are also designing spe-

Figure 1-1   Computer table (photo courtesy of Uarco, Inc.)

cial chairs. Figure 1-6 shows a typical chair designed specifically for data/word entry. The lever under the seat adjusts the seating height, as shown in Figure 1-7. Single chairs can be matched with all manners of support tables and desks (see Figure 1-8).

There are many other kinds of equipment designed to assist people who must work with computer terminals. Figure 1-9 is a typical copyholder for computer printouts and Figure 1-10 holds letter-size documents providing hands-free operation; the foot treadle allows the operator to advance or back up the document. Figure 1-11 shows a bracket-mounted copyholder for 8½ × 11 inch paper.

There are other furniture items and accessories that can enhance working conditions, but all the equipment in the world won't help if people aren't allowed to select their own break times. In Sweden, the government declared no one will work for more than two hours in front of a VDT without an opportunity to get away from that terminal for a short while.

12

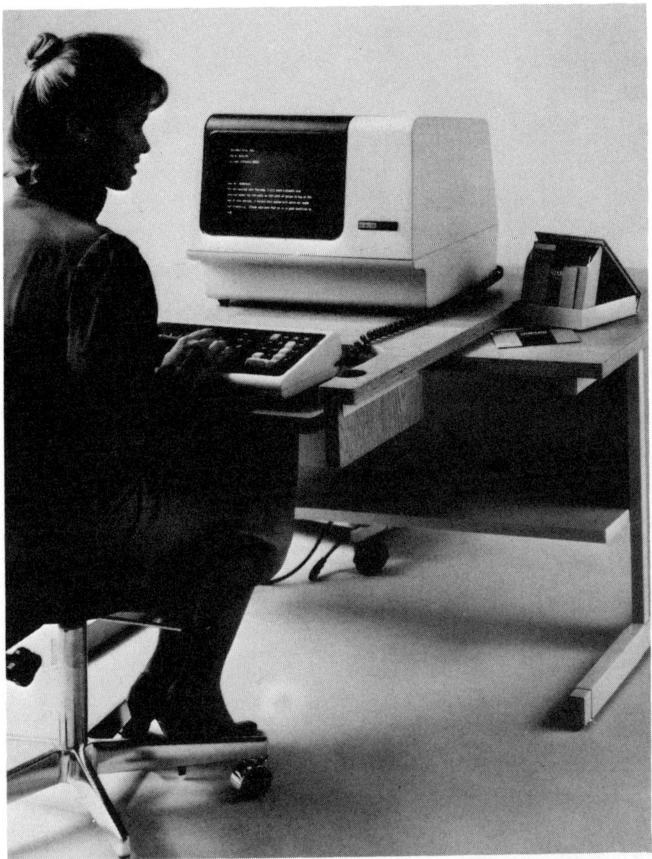

Figure 1-2   Table for detachable keyboard (photo courtesy of Uarco, Inc.)

Environmental Considerations

One of the biggest concerns people have about VDTs is the glare and other visually irritating conditions CRTs create. For some people, the glare and associated eyestrain is a secondary consideration; their primary concern is electromagnetic radiation emission. I've encountered a number of situations in which pregnant women refuse to use computer terminals during pregnancy. As far as most experts can determine, the stray emissions from a CRT aren't harmful to human health, but psychologists do warn us about human *beliefs* relative to health. If a person harbors a deep fear about the dangers of working with computer equipment, they'll greatly increase the probability that something negative will happen to them. Obviously, the fear arises from ignorance, and ignorance can normally be conquered through knowledge. Wisdom and knowledge build confidence that eliminates or reduces fear. That wis-

Figure 1-3   Computer desk (photo courtesy of Uarco, Inc.)

dom is part of a manager's responsibility. He or she must see to it that people are informed about the operation of computers, that their questions are fully answered, and that they are made to feel a part of what is going on.

Most CRT screens in use today are known as monochromatic—that is, they use a single color for display. The predominant color in use

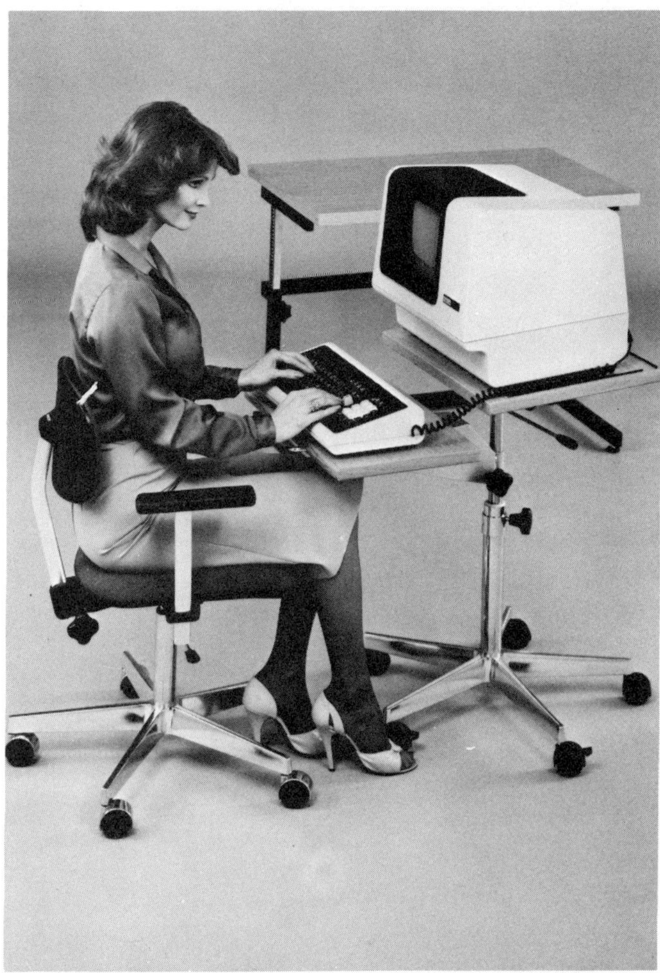

Figure 1-4   Computer desk (photo courtesy of Uarco, Inc.)

today is a light green. Multicolor screens, although visually dramatic, may present more of a potential problem than the monochromatics. This in no way suggests that they're hazardous, but their emissions are higher. Would you feel comfortable working twelve inches away from a color TV set all day?

Scandinavian countries have standard screens that present yellow characters on a dark brown background. Because the display is more soothing and easier to see, errors decrease as well as eyestrain. This yellow-on-brown screen is gaining popularity in the United States.

Glare does seem to be quite a problem; anyone who spends a full workday in front of a VDT can tell you about the eyestrain and possible accompanying headache that attends this kind of work. Fluorescent

Figure 1-5   Complete computer desk (photo courtesy of Uarco, Inc.)

lights seem to intensify the problem; this could be a result of the blinking effects of both the fluorescents and the screen itself. Fluorescent lights fluctuate more than incandescents; we've all seen fluorescent lamps on their last legs where the pulsating sensation becomes almost strobe-like. The human body doesn't respond well to pulsating light, and fluorescent lamps normally follow the sixty-cycle-per-second frequency of alternating current. (Incandescent bulbs also respond to the sixty-cycle fluctuations, but they're not as visible.) If you want to see the stroboscopic effects of fluorescent lighting, simply wave your hand back and

16

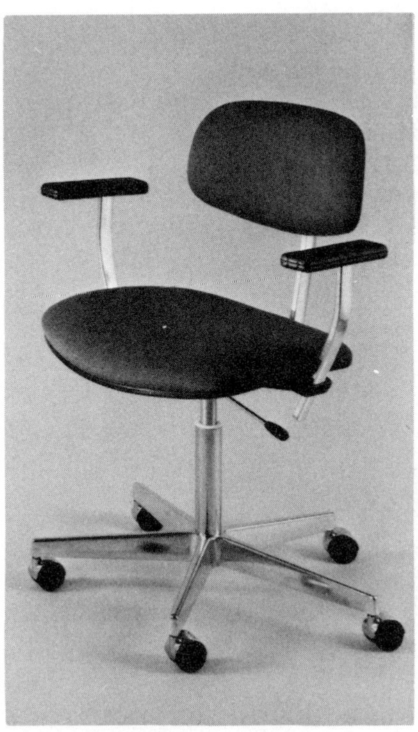

Figure 1-6 Ergonomic chair (photo courtesy of Uarco, Inc.)

Figure 1-7 Chair being adjusted (photo courtesy of Uarco, Inc.)

Figure 1-8 Matched chair and table (photo courtesy of Uarco, Inc.)

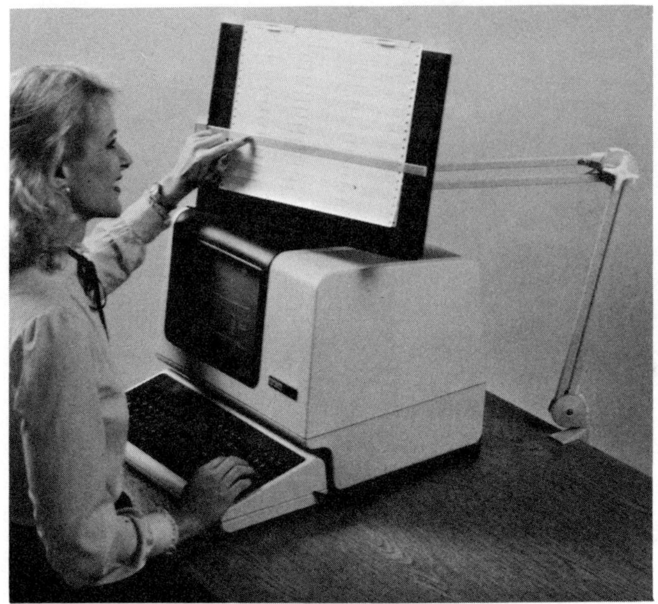

Figure 1-9   *Copyholder (photo courtesy of Uarco, Inc.)*

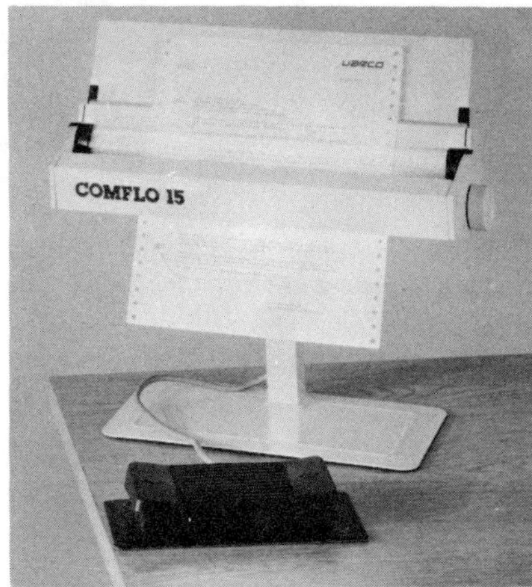

Figure 1-10   *Copyholder (photo courtesy of Uarco, Inc.)*

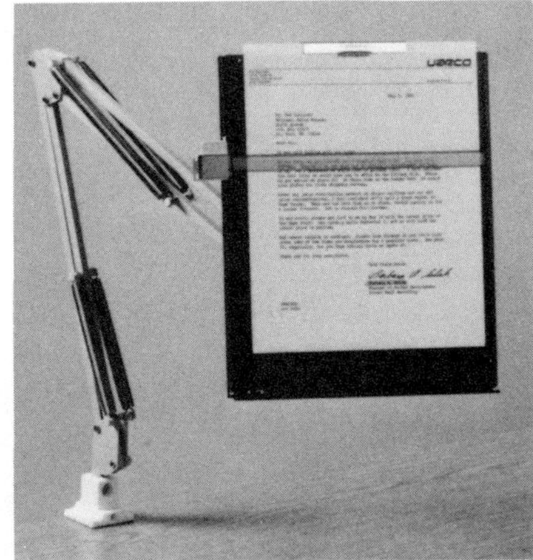

Figure 1-11   *Copyholder (photo courtesy of Uarco, Inc.)*

forth and watch your fingers. A VDT screen actually "blinks" several hundred times per second as the electron beam within the CRT writes and rewrites information on the phosphor screen. This out-of-phase condition between screen and room lighting can be quite disturbing visually and physiologically. Individual incandescent desk lamps lessen this visual disturbance.

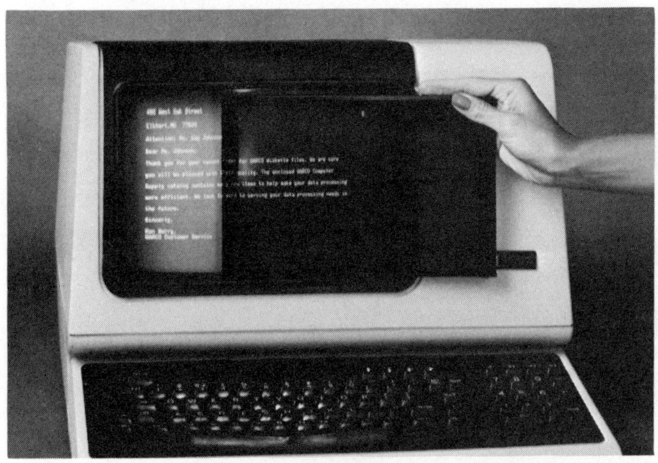

Figure 1-12   Anti-glare screen (photo courtesy of Uarco, Inc.)

It's surprising to walk around a normal office area and see the makeshift hoods and caps workers construct out of tape and cardboard to reduce overhead glare and reflection from general office lighting. Specially designed hoods are also available from many office- and computer-supply companies. One very simple alternative is to purchase antiglare screens (Figure 1-12) which operators say reduce eyestrain considerably. Screens of this type are available for most common terminals (Cado, IBM, DEC, Apple, NBI, Wang, H-P) and attach either with magnets or adhesive.

While we're discussing environmental factors affecting our computerized workplaces, let's look at a few other areas that cause discomfort. Many equipment operators and computer programmers complain about sounds that emanate from these machines. Unfortunately, some computer manufacturers design their equipment to sound like an arcade game with incessant beeping and whistling. Although using audible signals to focus the operator's attention may be a good idea, there can be too much of a good thing. If operators feel more comfortable with less sound there should be a way to eliminate or at least lessen either the number of beeps or the volume of the noise itself. Your equipment supplier can tell you whether or not this can be done with your present system or the one(s) you're considering.

Another noise that's bothersome is the sound that small printers make. People liken the sound to that of fingernails scraping on a blackboard, a noise that totally unnerves most people probably because of its resemblance to a human scream. The answer to bothersome printers is an acoustic cover. Figures 1-13 and 1-14 show two typical "hush covers," as they're commonly called. The more production printing that's done, the more the need to deaden the sound.

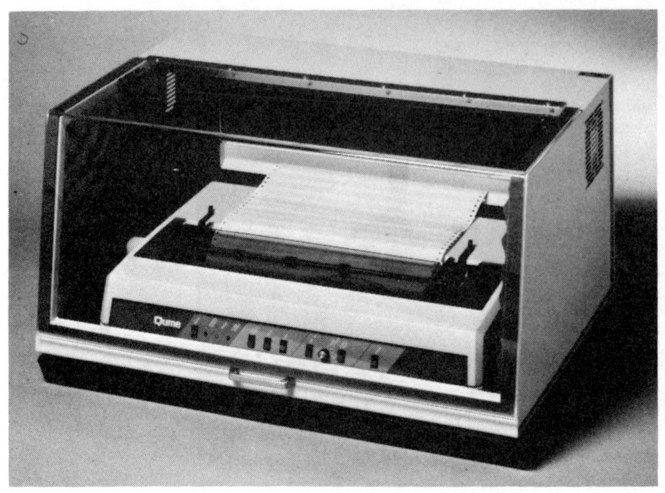

Figure 1-13   Hush cover (photo courtesy of Uarco, Inc.)

A rather interesting workplace problem is static electricity; sometimes uncomfortable shocks occur in a very dry office area, especially in the winter when the humidity is low. Of course, static electricity shocks aren't unique to computer equipment as any office worker will tell you—desks, chairs, file cabinets, even doors can deliver a healthy jolt in

Figure 1-14   Hush cover (photo courtesy of Uarco, Inc.)

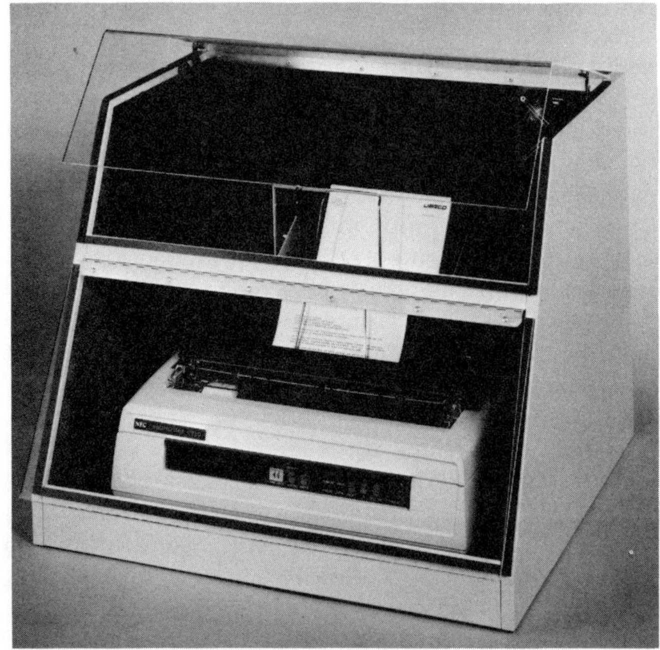

ousands of volts. The problem with some computer equip-
 e shock (or more correctly, the equalizing of electrical po-
 en human and machine) may also affect the machine,
 the addition or deletion of small amounts of information. The
 wer to this nagging problem is a special antistatic mat or carpet (refer
to Figure 1-1). You can also purchase more expensive clear plastic mats
as well as those that require grounding. The latter come with a wire for
attachment to the ground of an electrical outlet.

This initial focus is on the individual workplace in terms of furniture items and equipment accessories to lessen fatigue and physical discomfort. The philosophy of all this is simply—why not make it comfortable for people to do their work? If you don't care about working
conditions, then you don't care about people. Managers ponder why the
Japanese seem to be able to outstrip us in quality and price at the same
time. The answer is that Japanese management demonstrates care and
concern for the people who work in their businesses. That care and concern is directly reflected in worker performance, one byproduct of
which is greater sales and profits. People commit themselves to work
when they feel a part of it—and are told of their personal importance—
and they commit themselves to an organization when they feel they
truly belong. You demonstrate wisdom by communicating *and* listening,
and you demonstrate love by your genuine concern for people's well-
being and betterment and by making them feel wanted and appreciated.

Some of that concern is evident when you allow people to have a
voice in things that will affect them. That possibility brings me to a brief
discussion of office layout.

Office Layout

There's no perfect way to design the physical layout of individual and
collective workspaces because of the great variability between one individual and another. Some people prefer to work by themselves more
than with others, and the recognition of this principle of personal
choice should enter into office design. I suggest you have the equipment
users themselves design what they want, within the guidelines of expense, and to select the appropriate decor that reflects the overall
wishes of the group. If Fred wants posters stressing violent overthrow of
the government on the walls where he works, chances are the group
will bring peer pressure to bear on him and temper his poor judgment.

I don't want to show you how to design workspaces as much as
make you aware of a few principles. We seem to have created two extremes in workplace design in this country, neither of which is totally
effective. The first approach is to group people together and assign them
desks and chairs just as in elementary school. This dining-hall seating
arrangement has several drawbacks:

1. People treated like first-graders may indeed begin to act like first-grade.
2. People aren't highly motivated when involved in seating arrangemen
   over which they have no choice.
3. Such an arrangement gives an impression of regimentation, and fewer
   people than ever want to be regimented and made to look the same as
   others.

Much of the basic work with computers—data entry, typing on a word
processor, information inquiry—is dull, boring, and routine. It doesn't
help morale, productivity, and efficiency to have rows and columns of
people sitting at identical work stations. It's archaic and inefficient.

Recently I visited a major paper and cardboard manufacturer that
allows its data-processing people to plan within budgetary limits their
own overall workplace, including color selection for walls, panels, and
furniture. The department manager chose a corner workplace where his
people have ready access to him. Several people in the department
chose to have their own cubicles, and two groups formed small
clusters—a group of three and another group of five. The entire department also agreed to something quite creative; in one corner of the large
area that housed the people and the equipment, they placed a conference table, several comfortable chairs, and a VDT. This is used for breaks,
official meetings, or by groups of two or three people getting together in
what might be called neutral territory to discuss work-related situations.
The terminal is there so they have access to the central computer without needing to return to someone's desk.

The other extreme in office design is isolation—people shut away
from others. The situation is bad enough when executives demand pri-
vacy but use their office as a hideout; but deliberate isolation of workers
from one another in the name of efficiency is downright foolish. People
need one another. If you isolate people—and that includes isolation
from you—you face lowered morale, decreased productivity, high levels
of dissatisfaction, more mistakes, more expense. However, some people
require more space than others, and it's most important to keep their
preferences in mind. You still can set the limits; people don't mind that.
So, if terminals can't be separated from the central processor (as might
be the case with a shared-logic WP system) by more than, say, twenty
feet, to accommodate those workers who prefer to work alone, be sure to
tell them that. They'll work with it and within those constraints as long
as they've been told.

Cyberphobia: Computer Fear

We began this chapter with a discussion of health, and we'll end it with
the same subject. Professor Sanford B. Weinberg of St. Joseph University
in Philadelphia, Pennsylvania, estimates that 30 percent of American of-

fice workers are not comfortable with computer equipment or computer terminology.* One worker out of five, including managers, demonstrates actual fear symptoms when computers are brought into the workplace, and these symptoms include nausea, dizziness, vomiting, and stomachaches. This is not the physical discomfort we spoke of earlier (eyestrain, backaches, headaches) that might be thought of as a somatopsychic condition (bodily strain producing negative emotions). Cyberphobia is a true psychosomatic state in which the negative emotion of fear triggers unpleasant bodily responses.

Although some managers still believe in management by terror and surprise, fear produces one of three responses in humans and animals:

1. They will fight (insubordination, arguments).
2. They will freeze (inactivity, lack of momentum).
3. They will flee (stay home, quit, get fired).

None of these responses is desirable in our places of work. There may be only one basic fear—the fear a person holds that he or she will not be able to *cope* with some event. If people believe that they can't cope with something—like not being able to understand computer operations—they need to change their belief to one that convinces them they will be able to cope, understand, and even become highly skilled and proficient with computers.

Imagine that your young daughter has expressed a fear of water but still wants to learn to swim so that she can be with her friends. Would you take her to a deep lake or a rapidly flowing river and simply throw her in?

It's surprising the number of business owners, professionals in private practice, office managers, and executives who believe in the sink-or-swim approach for their people. Although most people enjoy a challenge, they don't particularly like facing the prospect of drowning. A "drowned" employee is not a satisfied, productive employee.

One major point to keep in mind about people and machines: Computers are invented by human beings, and their operation can be understood by human beings. It is neither wise nor caring to foist computer equipment on people without their involvement in its selection and adoption, and without training and information.

Just making changes will not, in the majority of cases, cause conditions to get better. Unilateral management-to-worker decisions often backfire because (1) the workers aren't involved in what's happening, and (2) the workers don't feel that anyone really cares about them as people.

*"Get Vertigo Over Video Displays?", *Wall Street Journal*, June 8, 1982.

It's wisdom and love, giving knowledge and caring. These are the *real* answers, the underlying philosophy. Tables, chairs, antiglare screens, and the like are important considerations to be sure, but in and of themselves they are not instant cures. They are the outward and visible signs of our inner and spiritual realization that people need to be loved.

Now that we've discussed the physical environment, let's examine the interaction between humans and computers.

Human-Machine Interaction

2

Software in General

By now, you should be aware that software is a term used to describe the commands or programs enabling a computer or a word processor to carry out its functions. This word is in contrast to hardware, which defines the physical pieces of equipment such as printers, disk drives, VDTs, and the like. For many years in the computer industry, it's been said that the capabilities of the hardware far outstrip software development. In other words, we could stop hardware innovations right now and it would take us several years to exploit fully the computing power of the existing hardware through enhanced software. Part of the current problem with software is that it's not interactive enough with the human operator; it simply does not consider the psychology of people. Much of the software in use today is cold, impersonal, lacking in flexibility, and in some cases downright threatening and insulting.

Humanizing our computer software, and giving more thought to the operators of the equipment, will necessarily become a more important issue in the future. A lot of this development must come from the system's programmers, the people who initially create the software. There have been some recent developments that make software softer, more human, but we have a long way to go to improve the interactions between humans and machine.

Let's look at some examples.

After being at his new job for three days, Harry begins to gain some familiarity with the computer terminal on his desk. He learns to access some of the programs that he'll be working with in the weeks and months to come. As Harry gains a modicum of confidence with the system, he experiments by entering some commands as well as some data. Suddenly the screen blanks out; then it sends a single message:

FATAL ERROR. PROGRAM TERMINATED.

That tersely worded phrase could certainly strike terror in the heart of a neophyte. The fear issue again raises its head. So Harry freezes. "Now what?" he asks. "*Fatal* means *death*. Did I kill the computer? Will I be canned for this?" Harry's new-found confidence ebbs.

How much easier the following message would have been to swallow:

YOU HAVE ATTEMPTED TO DIVIDE BY ZERO. THIS PROCESS WILL RESULT IN A CALCULATION THAT CAN'T BE CARRIED OUT. PLEASE PRESS "ESCAPE" TO RE-ENTER THE DATA OR TYPE A "1" TO BYPASS THE CALCULATION.

Myrna is a veterinarian. Recently, the animal hospital where she works acquired a computer system designed specifically for veterinary practices. Although she realizes the benefits of computerizing the practice, she's not very happy with the current system for one primary reason: In the past, Myrna prepared a written history of a visit by an animal (symptoms, diagnosis, prescribed treatment), but she also added other comments including, in many cases, information about the owner. The computer, in creating the patient record, allows only a few short fields for describing the conditions of the animal. Information about the patient must also be restricted to certain alphanumeric codes that bear no resemblance to the actual word used in veterinary medicine. For instance, for a dog that had a rabies vaccine, the proper code is not "RAB VAC", which could be easily understood, but "IM714".

The upshot of this is that she still keeps manual records and now has to prepare computer forms as well.

In this chapter we'll discuss problems that exist in some of our current software. It's important to be aware of some of the situations that arise because of problem software. Some of these can be overcome with little effort, but some may be irresolvable because your system is inflexible. For those experiencing the latter, take heart; you can do it better the next time around. Just being aware of a problem situation goes a long way toward making it better.

Friendly Software

We'll use the word *friendly* to cover a multitude of subjects involving humanizing computer software in terms of both the operator and the machine. The harder something is to use, the harder it is to get people to use it. Fewer people are willing to struggle through the learning process, and the time and expense required to bring those individuals to a point of proficiency will increase. There may also be many more errors along the way.

Interactive software is software that often asks questions:

DO YOU WISH TO SEE THE INCOME STATEMENT?
Y OR N?

It also presents choices using a table of alternate selections called a *menu*:

SALES ANALYSIS REPORTS AVAILABLE

1. SALES BY SALESPERSON, PAST 12 MONTHS
2. SALES BY REGION, PAST 12 MONTHS
3. SALES BY PRODUCT, YEAR-TO-DATE
4. MARKET SHARE, CURRENT QUARTER
5. GRAPH OF TOTAL SALES, PAST 24 MONTHS

PLEASE INDICATE CHOICE:

Although interactive software is commonplace today, it's important to keep in mind that software should not only be technically sound, meaning that it does the job it's supposed to, but it should also be geared to people. This holds true whether you're creating software within your own organization or purchasing packaged or canned software from an outside supplier.

In both cases, user involvement is vital. All too often systems analysts and programmers or in-house programming staffs create specific software for a department, sales for instance, debug the program, and hand it over to the department as a *fait accompli*. During the creation of the program, the computer department personnel spend a lot of time with the user department making certain that the software provides the right information; but few of these programmers ever sit with the operators, the people who will actually be using the system. Many times I've heard operators voice strong sentiment because they weren't involved in the development of the software. The same holds true for purchased software packages. Too often a department manager or a business owner looks for the least expensive program that will perform some task, like handling accounts receivable, but spends little or no time examining how the system may affect the people who must use the system. Again, if something is difficult to work with, worker dissatisfaction will increase; productivity and efficiency will decrease.

Software users as well as software developers must give more attention to the way operators prefer to work with computers. We all need to be more aware of how long it takes operators to perform certain tasks—move hand to keyboard, look at screen, reach for new data entry form. Essentially, this process involves some simple time and motion studies and should also take mental pauses into account.

Not only is there a lot of very unfriendly software on the market, there is software that forces people to work at a pace that may be strained or unnatural. All invididuals like to work at a rate that is best for them, and all people are different. If you combine threatening error messages ("DISASTROUS OVERFLOW", "JOB ABANDONED") with unnaturally paced software that offers the operator little opportunity for pauses and breaks, or software that contains no built-in routines to clarify and answer questions, you set up the conditions for a situation akin to a Detroit production line.

In a typical automobile assembly-line operation using humans rather than robots, a car chassis passes a worker in a fixed period of time. The worker is expected to perform some job like installing a window or bolting a fender as that auto assembly moves by. There is no room for variability, no opportunity to do the job differently. Many people become terribly frustrated or mentally dull themselves with drugs and alcohol. I don't think we need to repeat that mistake in our offices by forcing people to serve a machine that may even seem hostile in some cases. The auto worker is expected to do his or her job without question. The same is true in some computerized organizations today. The machines are essentially saying, "You do it my way or you will lose your job." Operators are expected to heed the commands of the computer and to follow its prescribed methods. There's no room for questions, little chance for individuality.

So, what are some solutions to these human-machine problems?

Helps and Prompts

Data General Corporation was one of the first computer companies to recognize that software not only needs to ask questions of operators (prompts), but that there also should be routines that provide explanations (helps).

Prompts such as "SYSTEM READY" or "PLEASE ENTER TODAY'S DATE" have been around for some time and software designers are now well-convinced of their value, but some software systems may contain few of them and other systems may use unfriendly messages. An unfriendly message may take several forms:

1. Imperative commands such as "ENTER DATA NOW" or "WAIT. SYSTEM BUSY". These cold and impersonal messages may frustrate, confound, and confuse. Rather than issuing orders to an operator, software should announce that the system is awaiting the operator at his or her convenience. Few people like to be ordered to do things, especially if that order is issued by a machine. The "READY" type of message is far preferable to one that commands. Users should feel they're in control, not the computer.

2. Hostile messages. Words such as "CATASTROPHIC", "ERROR", "IL-LEGAL", "INVALID", "FATAL", "ABORTED", "DISASTROUS", "ABANDONED", "REJECTED" should not be used. Compare

"ILLEGAL ENTRY, COMMAND REJECTED".

to

"PUT COMMAND REQUIRES A COMMA".

3. Obscure messages and commands. Programmers have their own language like any professionals, but when they assume that laypeople automatically know what they're talking about, they may be mistaken. Sometimes messages speak in computerese, like

"EOF REACHED AT LINE 14701".

or

"IMPROPERLY NESTED LOOPS".

or even

"SYN ERR REJ 1742018792".

Messages designed to inform operators should do just that. When people don't understand what's going on, their fears about computerization are heightened.

4. Messages that are too general. When a VDT responds with "WHAT?" or "WRONG DATA", most operators feel extremely frustrated unless they're very familiar with the system. Newer operators may be totally paralyzed. I watched a young man dealing with a computer system that kept responding "WHAT?" to his attempts to bypass that message. He ended his unsuccessful attempts to get by the childlike, repetitive questioning with a string of obscenities, and stormed off.

Some computer systems respond to operator mistakes with something like

"ERROR NO. 47".

When this cryptic comment appears on the screen, the operator must consult a written manual. It's better to have a machine that responds with

"YOU HAVE OMITTED A LEFT PARENTHESIS IN THE LAST ENTRY".

Programmers in the distant past (circa 1965) said messages had to be few and short because computer memory was so expensive. With today's larger memories, this claim is no longer valid.

A help routine within a computer system is just what the name implies. Software designers who keep the operator in mind build in explanations giving needed information. When people question terms or routines that the computer system is using, the machine may periodically ask

"NEED HELP? Y OR N?"

or the operator may type in "HELP" or "?" at various points.

Let's watch a person working with a computer program that handles auto insurance claims. Operator entries will be underlined. The operator first enters the proper codes for the claim program and the machine responds

SYSTEM READY. PLEASE ENTER TYPE OF CLAIM.

    1. FIRE OR THEFT LOSS
    2. COLLISION—SINGLE VEHICLE
    3. PROPERTY DAMAGE TO OTHER VEHICLE
    4. DAMAGE TO PROPERTY OTHER THAN VEHICLE
    5. PERSONAL LIABILITY
    6. OTHER

Operator responds:

> <u>1</u>

FIRE OR THEFT LOSS? F OR T?

> <u>HELP</u>

FIRE LOSS TO A VEHICLE MEANS THAT A FIRE BEGAN WITHIN THE VEHICLE, OFTEN FROM AN ELECTRICAL SHORT CIRCUIT OR A SPARK IN THE GAS TANK. FIRE DAMAGE CAN ALSO BE CAUSED AS A RESULT OF THE VEHICLE BEING IN OR NEAR A FIRE OF ANOTHER ORIGIN, LIKE BEING IN A GARAGE THAT CAUGHT FIRE. THEFT OF A VEHICLE MEANS THE UNLAWFUL TAKING BY SOME-ONE NOT AUTHORIZED BY THE OWNER. THEFTS MUST BE REPORTED TO THE STATE POLICE IN THE STATE OF RESIDENCE OF THE INSURED AND CLAIMS CANNOT BE MADE UNTIL SEVEN DAYS AFTER DATE VEHICLE WAS STOLEN IF VEHICLE HAS NOT BEEN RECOVERED. IF A VEHICLE IS STOLEN AND <u>THEN</u> BURNS, IT IS CALLED A THEFT FOR INSURANCE PURPOSES.
DO YOU WISH MORE HELP? Y OR N?

> <u>N</u>

FIRE OR THEFT LOSS? F OR T?

> <u>F</u>

FIRE LOSS OF VEHICLE
ENTER NAME OF INSURED

> <u>ROBERT JOHNSON</u>

THIS PROGRAM REQUIRES THE LAST NAME OF THE IN-SURED TYPED FIRST, THEN A COMMA, FOLLOWED BY FIRST NAMES AND MIDDLE INITIAL. PLEASE RE-ENTER.

> <u>JOHNSON, ROBERT F.</u>

PLEASE ENTER POLICY NUMBER.

> <u>1074826-8</u>

THE CHECK DIGIT DOES NOT COMPUTE. PLEASE EXAM-INE THE POLICY NUMBER AGAIN AND RE-ENTER.

> <u>HELP.</u>

A CHECK DIGIT IS THE FINAL DIGIT IN THE POLICY NUM-BER, THE ONE FOLLOWING THE DASH. IT IS USED TO

VERIFY THE POLICY NUMBER. WE USE THE FOLLOWING RULE FOR CHECK DIGITS: ALL NUMBERS OF THE POLICY NUMBER ARE ADDED TOGETHER, THE TEN DIGIT IS DISCARDED, AND THE UNIT'S DIGIT IS THEN SUBTRACTED FROM ELEVEN. THIS IS CALLED MODULO 11 BY MATHEMATICIANS.

EXAMPLE: POLICY NUMBER 2137940-?

2 + 1 + 3 + 7 + 9 + 4 + 0 = 26. WE USE ONLY THE 6.

11 MINUS 6 = 5

THUS THE POLICY NO. WITH CHECK DIGIT INCLUDED IS 2137940-5. IS THIS CLEAR? Y OR N?

<u>N</u>

OK. PLEASE ENTER ONLY THE FIRST SEVEN DIGITS OF THE POLICY NUMBER THAT YOU ENTERED BEFORE.

<u>1074826</u>

VERY GOOD. NOW THE CHECK DIGIT FOR THIS NUMBER IS FOUND LIKE THIS:

1 + 0 + 7 + 4 + 8 + 2 + 6 = 28

11 − 8 = 3

THE POLICY NUMBER IN FULL IS 1074826-3.

OK TO CONTINUE? Y OR N?

<u>Y</u>

DATA MATCHES.

POLICYHOLDER: JOHNSON, ROBERT F.

POLICY NO.: 1074826-3

PLEASE ENTER VEHICLE SERIAL NUMBER

Here you see how help routines within help routines teach the operator (for example, explain how a check digit is calculated) in addition to helping the operator supply the correct information.

Some organizations are experimenting with voice output for help routines. There will undoubtedly be more of this in the future, and the general feeling is that a voice is more friendly than codes or a screen; however, care must be used before wholesale, across-the-board adoption is made. The spoken word, even a computer-spoken word, is fleeting and may have to be repeated if an operator misses it.

There is no reason why helps, prompts, error messages, system status displays, and the like have to be formal. Most people prefer informal-ity and even some light humor. One university program for student instruction that I ran had messages like:

It shouldn't be overdone, though. Some computer departments have done things like print a picture of Snoopy or Alfred E. Neuman when an operator makes a mistake. The first time, it's funny. After the twentieth printout, the humor is lost.

Delays and Interruptions

There are short delays lasting several seconds and long delays that may go on for minutes. The short delays are more frequent and any operator who has worked with a VDT is very familiar with them. Delays usually occur because the computer is processing information or looking for something in a file. Most computer systems are designed to present data on the screen as soon as the short task is completed. The problem with this is twofold:

1. The time involved in delays can vary considerably.
2. The operator often has no idea how long he or she will have to wait for delays longer than a few seconds.

Although there's some controversy, most operators prefer a uniform delay because of their desire to maintain a natural working rhythm. Operators complain that when they deal with a delay of one second, followed by a delay of ten seconds and then one of five seconds, they're unable to establish a working pattern. Any pace they try to establish is thrown off. With an irregular pace, they tire more easily and are prone to more mistakes. Some innovative organizations are working toward providing uniform delays. In such systems, the information may be held back for several seconds so that the computer can produce a longer but uniform delay.

For example, an organization finds that 90 percent of the short-term, waiting-type delays occur within a ten-second range. They then design in variable delays to make the total waiting time ten seconds. Of course, 10 percent of the delays would take more than ten seconds, but more of a pattern is established because operators know what to expect. There is also a message on the VDT that informs the operator that a standard delay is being used while the computer processes information or searches the files. Remember the computer on board the spaceship *Enterprise* in the television series *Star Trek* that informs Captain Kirk or Mr. Spock that it's "working" before it presents its information? That's a standard delay.

In the case of longer delays of twenty seconds or more, some computer systems may be able to so inform the operator. Although it's not totally necessary to tell someone exactly how long they might have to wait, classes of delays may be specified; for example:

    Class 1: 20 to 40 seconds
    Class 2: 40 to 60 seconds
    Class 3: 1 to 2 minutes
    Class 4: Longer than 2 minutes

The computer system might even use a hierarchy of messages like the ones above and "drop down" in class level as it nears the completion of a task. If, for instance, the machine initially informs an operator that there will be a Class 4 delay, it switches to a Class 3 delay when the time to completion becomes less than two minutes.

The question then arises about what to do during these longer delays. It's my personal feeling that workers should be free to do what they want—get a cup of coffee, do other work, or even use the computer for something else like playing a game.

There are a number of organizations that have purchased or developed computer games, appealing graphics displays, music, or other pastimes for operators to give them a break in their work, especially if the computer is delayed for a while. Some managers fear that this kind of activity is frivolous and has no place at work. Work, they reason, is a serious matter and fun is to be discouraged. They also fear that productivity will slip and that their workforce will do nothing but play games. In other words, these managers believe that their people will take advantage of recreational computing if it is offered.

By and large people respond as a function of how they are treated. If you treat them like children, they behave like children. If you treat them like responsible adults, capable of selecting their own pace throughout the day, that is how they behave. Having fun is normal and does not generally detract from efficiency; it adds to it. If you keep your workers informed and involved and demonstrate that you truly care for them as people and not just as individuals performing some dull, boring, routine task, most will work toward your chosen goals.

Interruptions in your business are another matter to consider when selecting or designing software. People are interrupted all the time at work for meetings, phone calls, and requests to perform some task other than what they are working on.

John G. Kreifeldt, professor of design at Tufts University, performed a very interesting test studying interruptions and the ability of people to return quickly and efficiently to what they were doing before the interruption occurred. He tested two groups of individuals—each group was equipped with a different brand of calculator. One calculator uses algebraic notation and the other brand uses reverse Polish notation (no equal sign on the keyboard). He gave the two groups identical sets of problems to solve and then interrupted the groups for about twenty-second intervals. After the interruption, the subjects returned to their work.

After the test was over, Professor Kreifeldt discovered that the group with the reverse Polish calculators were able to recover much more quickly from the interruption. The reason has to do with the way that such calculators display information; they give the operator more of a clue as to where they left off.

Although calculators are much different from computers, the lesson from this brief test is clear. If the software is obscure in the way it interacts with people, interruptions may have a dual effect in terms of time lost on a particular job—there's the time involved with the interruption itself and the time it takes the operator to recover and return to work.

If a particular operator uses a routine on a repetitive basis, the interruption-recovery problem is not as profound. For seldom-used programs and those that are long and involved, the matter of recovery is more important.

If you're in the process of purchasing software from an outside vendor, be sure to ask about interruptions. If you already have software installed, it might be worthwhile to discuss with your people the effect interruptions have on it. If it's a significant problem, the software can always be changed. People returning to a job need to know where they left off. Sometimes this can be accomplished by having the program restructure the job for the operator:

THE LAST ENTRY MADE WAS THE LABOR EXPENSE FOR MAY 1984 FOR THE ASSEMBLY DEPT. THE AMOUNT YOU ENTERED WAS

$21,240.00

TYPE A "1" TO CONTINUE OR A "2" IF YOU WISH TO SEE PREVIOUS ENTRIES.

Restrictive Software

Restrictive software includes programs that:

1. Do not match the way the organization actually does business.
2. Force users to adopt certain codes or fields that are unnatural or confusing to them.

Often these two problems go hand-in-hand. Both create a basic problem by taking an existing way of doing things and then "shoehorning" that business method into the same software system. In the 1960s, big business began making basic mistakes in acquiring computer systems. They spent several million dollars on a computer, built special rooms to house and cool it, hired a roomful of people to serve their new god, and then looked around for something for it to do. After a year or two, they could grind out the company's payroll, possibly saving the wage of a couple of $60-per-week payroll clerks. Such companies and other organizations also heeded the words of IBM and others who convinced them that they must have this wonderful technology and that the computer companies had all the answers, including, in some cases, how their customer should run his or her business. Organizations changed the ways that they were doing things and, although some of these changes were beneficial, others were disastrous.

There are many quasimythical stories about computer systems and the problems they've caused. One story concerns a major U.S. manufacturer of electrical motors. The marketing department decided that the company should no longer sell very small fractional-horsepower motors, and so over a weekend they had the existing inventory of these motors hauled away to a major wholesaler for a distress-price sale. On Monday, the inventory clerk dutifully noted that there were no motors in stock. When the computer got its hand on this information and did the "proper" calculations, it signalled the production department that an out-of-stock condition existed. "Better make more motors," it ordered. The factory geared up for the production of something that was no longer needed and was soon running at full bore before someone caught the mistake. Now, certainly, we could point to a lack of communication between marketing and production, but the story is meant to emphasize what can happen.

Today too many organizations select computer systems and software without giving much thought as to how they do business now and/or how they want to do business in the future. The problem of restricted software is much more prevalent in purchased software than developed software. A small business or department within a larger organization often tries to find the least expensive hardware and software combination and then winds up having to "do business" the way the software does business.

I'm not speaking so much about standard word processors or devices that simply provide a faster way to type, but about business, nonprofit, and government groups that look for new computer systems before they decide what they want such a system to do. First, track how data moves within your organization, decide what information and reports you want from that data, and then look for or develop systems that provide what *you* want. If you have to adapt your operation to accommodate the system, you've lost some control of your own business. I'm not against making changes to increase efficiency, but I am against making changes simply to conform to a computer program. Smaller organizations—small businesses, banks, town governments, schools—too often fall victim to what is called a turnkey system, a hardware/ software combination that is delivered ready to run. They discover too late that they must fit themselves to the computer rather than the reverse.

Planning what you want in advance eliminates much of this problem. Plan what you and your people want from a computer system and then investigate what is available. Be leery of packaged software that cannot be changed. If you lock yourself into an inflexible system, you may find yourself in the market for additional or even completely different software after a very frustrating period.

Earlier in this section we said that some programs severely restrict the kind or amount of information that can be entered and stored. This is another holdover from the days of limited computer memory when short codes were used for practically everything. There's nothing wrong with codes as long as those codes have meaning to the users. Beware of reducing normal words and phrases (accounts receivable, demand note, viral infection) to meaningless alphanumeric codes (M704, 27BCZ) that only create confusion and necessitate time-consuming cross-reference. Either be certain that the length of the field can accommodate words the way you use them or, if abbreviations are necessary, construct them in a way that people can easily understand—ACCTREC, DEMNOTE, VIRLINF.

Security

One topic that comes up repeatedly is software and data security. Security refers to the built-in protection that organizations developed to keep unauthorized users from accessing certain information. It is my view that most defensive countermeasures are totally unnecessary. I receive severe criticism for my ideas on this subject and the argument that is leveled at me is that I'm not aware of the reality of the situation. "Don't you realize," people ask me, "what can happen if one of our clerical people gets into the customer file or has access to financial information?" My usual answer is, "So what? What are you so afraid of? And, more importantly, why do you distrust your people so much?"

If someone really wants to gain access to something, they'll find a way to do it, security system or not. One manufacturing company I visited recently has five or six levels of codes, some of which change daily. They also have a program that informs some supervisor somewhere if an individual makes more than three unsuccessful attempts to get through these codes. Imagine—a computer that rats on people! When I asked the data-processing people what information they so vitally wanted to protect, it was things like production levels and inventory status. They wanted to hide this information from their own people!

An overemphasis on security means you don't trust the very people whom you have hired, and that means you don't trust yourself. The only way you can ascribe a quality like lack of trust to someone else is if you feel that way about yourself—it takes one to know one, as kids will say. The great majority of people, 95 percent and maybe even more, respond in a trustworthy fashion if they feel that they are trusted. A lot of Pentagon-type security only demonstrates your lack of trust and confidence *in yourself.*

I'm not telling you that there may be something such as payroll information that you might want to keep restricted. Although there's no good reason why wage and salary data has to be secretive, right now we still are a bit fearful about total openness in this area. Some organizations already choose to operate in a way that everyone knows what everyone else makes and this may represent a coming change, but it will probably be a very gradual one.

The point I want to make is that much attention, time, and money can be wasted trying to prevent that one-in-a-thousand chance that someone will break into a computer system and do something harmful. The answer to this fear is not greater, more intricate security systems; once again, the answer is love and wisdom. If people feel they belong and are truly important (love), and are told about things that affect them individually and collectively (wisdom), the need for tight security disappears.

You get what you concentrate on. If you focus on building a workforce of caring, concerned, and informed people, you must demonstrate those qualities yourself. If you focus on something that your employees believe means you don't care or you aren't concerned about them, you may reap the results of that harvest. Focus on the people themselves, not on ways that show you distrust them. System security is needed only if people are dissatisfied. If you build in dissatisfaction and have no intention of working to lessen it, you'll need to have a security system.

Ask yourself this question: Do you honestly believe that fear works? Does it work for you?

Summary

The message of this chapter is a relatively simple one: Pay attention to the kind of software that you're using or that you intend to use. Make certain that the users are involved in its design, selection, and testing. Involve them in the changes that are going to take place because change can be intimidating, even frightening. If change, especially change involving computers, is not managed carefully with concern for all who will be affected by it, it produces few of the results you want and a host of those you don't. In Chapter 3, we'll explore change itself.

Technological Change

3

The Nature of Change

It has been said that the only two certain things in our world are death and taxes. But there are many other certainties in our world, and one of them is change. Everything changes. About every seven years all the cells in your body are replaced. Even physical constants in science change. There are new theories in physics that suggest that the speed of light, once fixed at 186,283 miles per second, varies. New York City undergoes regular changes as older buildings give way to new ones. Our social values are vastly different from one generation to another. A man or woman now ninety years old can relate stories of change the likes of which no one before them could even imagine. The only way no change occurs is if every conscious being chooses to define everything as perfect. Perfection, then, could be a curse rather than a blessing, because no growth, learning, or change would occur.

People fear change, or more correctly they fear the imagined consequences of that change. They fear that one way or another the outcome will make them lesser of a human being. For example, clerical workers may see office automation as a threat to their job. If they lose their job, they won't be able to pay the rent. That means they could be thrown into the street by a merciless landlord. They might have to beg friends and relatives for money and that would be self-debasing. And on and on.

In his second law of motion, Sir Isaac Newton postulated that an object traveling in a straight line will contunie to do so until acted on by an outside force. The same may be said for many people. Unfortunately, some managers feel that the outside force should be a threat—"If you don't do what I tell you to do, I'll fire you." A force can work in two ways—attraction and repulsion. The attractive force, as opposed to the repulsive one, presents the benefits of a particular change rather than stressing or implying what might happen to people if they don't adopt the change.

We are well used to change in our daily lives and recognize that some changes take longer to accomplish than others. Also, we must recognize that each person sees the *need* for change differently. Look at hair styles, especially for men. After the Beatles made their debut in the early 1960s, many men chose to wear their hair longer, but some stayed with the shorter style of the 1950s. The need to change varies from one person to another; some people rush from fad to fad, while others maintain essentially the same lifestyle from one year to another.

Agents of Change in a Technological Era

You are an agent of change. As a manager, business owner or professional, you cause things to happen. It's part and parcel of what you have chosen to do in your life. You were hired and promoted to institute and manage change. However, some organizations try to hold onto things the way they are and don't want to be told to do things differently. Many businesses that fail do so because they don't want to change. I once saw three established retail businesses fail over the course of three months in a bustling and growing Vermont town. Those of us who watched these businesses in their final death throes of reduced prices and clearance sales remarked that the only reason they failed was their inability to adapt to a changing world. They were all doing business the way they did it in the 1950s, and this was thirty years later.

On the opposite end of the spectrum are organizations that jump on every new fad that comes along. This be-the-first-on-your-block syndrome gets people dashing about without much real thought or planning. One of my favorite pieces of advice to potential agents of change is this brief rhyme:

> Be not the first
> By whom the new is tried;
> Nor yet the last
> To lay the old aside.

Of all the changes taking place in our complex world, technological change is often the most difficult. It's one thing to decide to wear your hair differently or buy a new wardrobe; it's quite something else to adopt new methods and new machinery that affect many people. People will willingly make changes if they believe the results of those changes will be beneficial. One of your tasks as an agent of change is to explain change in such a way that the change creates benefits rather than fear. What, then, are some of the fears that people have about using computers?

Certainly one fear is that the computer will disrupt the general order of things, an order that may have taken years to establish. I had an opportunity to sit with Wally Samuelson, the president of a small manufacturing company, while a salesman from a large computer company was making his pitch about the glories of his company's newest processor. After listening for half an hour, Wally asked the salesman for a specific example of how the computer would be more valuable. The salesman launched into a lengthy discussion of how the president could use the machine to tell him the status of orders within the factory. He stressed "real-time" information and how important it is for the president to be aware of what's happening now as opposed to what had happened in the past.

"You mean," the president asked, "that the computer could, for instance, tell me when particular orders, especially ones that are already late, will ship to the customer?"

"Precisely," answered the salesman. "Computers can supply you up-to-the-minute reports with great speed and accuracy. You certainly don't have that now."

"Oh, yeah?" said Wally. "Watch this." He flipped a switch on the intercom.

"Hey, Stanley. That you?"

"Yeah. Hi, Wally."

"Hi, Stan. Say, when's that RCA order going to ship?"

"Friday morning, sure thing."

"Can I tell the customer that?"

"Yeah, Wally, I'm as certain as I can be."

"Great. I really appreciate your attention to that. They can be real *@!?#s if we're more than two weeks late. Say, how's Helen?"

"Feeling better. Doctors are encouraged and so's she."

"Joyce?"

"It's been tough, but kids these days are very adaptive."

"Yeah, they also seem to be cuter than we were—than *you* were, anyway."

"Thanks, Wally, thanks. Anything else I can do for you?"

"Nope. That's it. Thanks again." Wally then pointed out three things to the computer peddler:

1. He not only got the information he needed, but some personal reassur-
   ance about it.
2. He was able to convey appreciation for the work that Stanley did, and to
   kid with him a bit.
3. He was able to ask about Stanley's wife, Helen, who recently underwent a
   touch-and-go operation. He was truly concerned about the situation.

Needless to say, the salesman didn't get the sale. *Sic transit gloria* computer peddler.

My point in this story is that Wally has evolved a certain *modus operandi* with his people. It's cordial, humanistic, and informative. He just didn't want or need a computer stuck between him and his subordinates.

If people fear disruption, it means that they believe the changes will not be beneficial. People often use the grapevine to discover inside information that will actually help them do their jobs more efficiently. Contrary to popular belief, grapevines are more accurate and more rapid than official channels, and they're quite healthy and natural. People may fear the disruption caused by computers will destroy their former routines, including communication, with other people. They also may believe that what they have now is fine; they figured it out themselves, and it works. In any case, it's important for you to recognize that many people don't want to disturb the order of things and it may take a concentrated effort on your part to describe fully any changes that you have in mind long before they occur. Give people time to think through how they can participate in the change, and they will willingly help you.

Another fear that people have regarding technological change is that they will not be able to grasp the new concepts and as a result will

1. Look dumb
2. Lose status and individuality
3. Be relegated to serving a machine
4. Lose their job
5. Experience all of the above in sequence.

People don't like to look stupid. Surely you remember a time when you were publicly embarrassed because you assumed you were doing something correctly only to be told there was a much different way, a much better way. Proper communication can usually solve the looking-dumb problem.

Between high school and college, my dad landed me a summer job with the highway department of the Commonwealth of Massachusetts. On my third day at the job, a crew of us were doing patchwork with hot asphalt on a highway outside of Boston. We finished our work in the afternoon and the foreman presented me with a large collection of rakes, shovels, brooms, and hoes, as well as a can of gasoline. Before he got into his pickup and drove away, he issued a curt order. "Smith," he said, "burn the tools," and vanished. After thinking over what he said and looking at what I had been given, I decided to take him literally. I gathered up some dry leaves and sticks, piled all the tools on top, poured gasoline over the entire mess, and threw a match to it all, creating a nice big fire.

Sometime later the foreman returned. What greeted him was a smoldering lump of ashes with the metal ends of the rakes, hoes, and shovels now sans handles. He couldn't believe it. First his face got red, then the veins in his neck stood out, and finally he hurled a string of unprintable epithets at me. Through his rage, I learned of my shortcomings and was made to consider some possibilities relevant to the legitimacy of my birth, but I also learned that "burn the tools" in highway talk means to pour gasoline onto the *metal* parts of the tools and allow the encrusted asphalt to burn away, leaving the metal clean once more. I felt dumb. I also felt broke for a couple of weeks because I had to reimburse the state—their insurance covered acts of God but not the acts of fools. "If only I had asked," I reflected many times later.

People can easily wind up looking dumb if they're not given the opportunity to learn and ask questions. Too many managers, in the name of what they believe is efficiency, drop a computer or a VDT in front of someone and say, "Here." Naturally, confusion follows. Some people try to stumble through, whereas others openly resist.

There are some people in the workforce who simply don't feel comfortable with machines. Their reasons are many and varied, but are valid to them. Many school systems are mandating that all teachers gain what they call computer literacy. I have some doubts whether this is wise. What about the 55-year-old English teacher who does such a marvelous job introducing youngsters to the classics, or her colleague who puts real life into the important events in history? Should they be forced to pass through some prescribed course of study to keep their jobs? Will they feel excitement or animosity? Methinks the latter.

You can't assume that everyone's the same. It's part of your responsibility to be attuned to individual differences, especially in a technological environment. There may be some people who don't want to learn about and use computers. If you value their other skills, you may have to help find something else for them to do. For people who see themselves as slaves to a machine, it's important to point out that the computer is a modern tool of business and should never be thought of as supplanting humans, only assisting them.

Another fear that people have is that they'll lose their individuality. One of the popular magazines in the United States advertises for new subscriptions on television and, to impress the viewer with how efficiently incoming telephone calls will be handled on a toll-free number, shows a massive room filled with men and women sitting at identical desks all a prescribed distance apart with VDTs on each desk. *They* call it efficiency, *I* call it an abomination.

In a May 6, 1983, article in the *Wall Street Journal* entitled "Terminal Tedium," staff reporter John Andrew cites three specific cases where large-scale office automation has produced anything but worker satisfaction. At Blue Shield in Plymouth, Massachusetts, American Express Company's southern Regional Operating Center in Plantation, Florida, and Equitable Life's Syracuse, New York, facility, workers feel that they have been depersonalized and controlled by the machines. At Blue Shield and American Express, the computer systems monitor human performance and issue efficiency reports that compare how long a report or a procedure should have taken versus the actual time that it did take. Such a reporting scheme causes nothing but ill will and probably harms overall performance more than it helps. Apparently we still haven't learned our lessons that people cannot be treated as some amorphous collection of similar beings. People are individuals, each highly unique.

The biggest fear of all, however, is the fear of losing one's job. It is a double fear: The first fear is of being sacked and the second one is of being thrown out into the street without a marketable talent because "everybody knows about computers." While it's true that our workforce changes over the years in terms of what people do, the computer has created more jobs than it's destroyed. People need to realize that they should continually upgrade their skills in this age of information, but this can be done in positive and rewarding ways. Most people want to grow and learn, but when they perceive that there's no benefit to them, they'll resist. From the beginning, it's important to emphasize that computers are not being used to do away with people. As a manager or business owner, you can stress the following:

1. New technologies mean new challenges; problem solving can actually be fun rather than tedious. New knowledge means an increase in personal wisdom, a wider field of skills, even greater marketability in the new job area.

2. Today, people connected with computers enjoy status and recognition among others in the workforce.

3. People in the computer field have the opportunity to earn above-average salaries, and because of their knowledge they are more likely candidates for advancement and promotion.

It's far better to approach any change, but especially technological change, from the standpoint of how people can be better off. You're not lying or psyching them up with false hope. You, as an agent of change, are demonstrating your belief in the advantages of the changes and are showing that you are truly concerned for the welfare of the people who will be most affected—those same people who have the most direct effect on the efficiency of your organization.

Human Mechanics and Change

The concept of inertia is well known in physics and engineering. A body will remain at rest until acted on by some force. This force is greater to begin the initial motion than that required to keep it moving. Albert Einstein, in discussing the photoelectric effect, also spoke of something called the streaming effect. In the human perception of sound, there is something called the threshold level that must be surpassed first before sound is heard. Human beings, dealing with their beliefs about themselves and the world that they perceive, often require a greater "force" or energy to begin them moving in some new direction than that required to keep them moving once underway. If workers believe that things are fine the way they are, you first need to mobilize the energy of your own belief that things may be fine, but they could be better. Then, you need to communicate that belief to others. If you don't possess sufficient potential (call it conviction if you want), you won't be successful in producing change. I don't mean that you should get yourself all pumped up and then hold meetings that are more like pregame pep rallies than information sessions. The half-time, locker-room approach has a particular, and somewhat fleeting, effect. Let's follow a hypothetical example of how technological change might be accomplished.

John Sykes is the CEO and owner of a medium-size plumbing and building supply wholesaling business, Stratford Distributors, Inc. The company has had a computer system for the past ten years that has handled inventory control and general accounting functions. John began thinking of a new computer system after attending a seminar, doing some reading, and talking with some of his colleagues. He wants to have nearly all Stratford personnel use the computer for such tasks as inventory, customer service, purchasing, billing, word processing, and electronic filing. Stratford employs twenty-three people, most of whom have had little experience with computers.

John first lays out the steps he believes will be necessary to make the transition to the new system. His general outline is as follows:

1. Discussions with managers and employees.
2. Establishment of an ad-hoc committee of five to six people.
3. Review of overall requirements by department.
4. Feasibility and applications study.
5. Contacting of vendors. Possible preparation of RFQ.
6. Review of hardware and software.

7. System selection.
8. Planning of installation with vendor and staff.
9. Training of all personnel.
10. Actual system installation.
11. Implementation of software.
12. Analysis and feedback.

After looking over his list off and on for a few days, he calls his three department managers together. Leo Burke is in charge of warehouse operations; Mary Manchester runs administration, which includes the present computer; and Sherri Wilkinson heads up sales and customer service. John gives them his basic ideas for the new system and tells them how he believes the machine will affect their areas. Leo will have the purchasing, receiving, inventory, and shipping system he's asked for, and Sherri's people could respond to customer inquiries more rapidly and accurately. Both of these individuals are quite excited about the idea, but Mary's skeptical, even a bit hostile. John quickly recognizes that her slight animosity stems from her perception that she would no longer have total responsibility for the computer because all employees would be involved in the new system. He reassures her that her role in the organization would not diminish, but that her responsibilities would actually grow. John tells her that he wants her to organize and oversee the ad-hoc computer committee. He suggests she select at least one person from each of the three departments, plus whomever else she feels can give valid input. Mary's fears quickly fade.

John discusses his list of tasks with Leo, Mary, and Sherri, and Leo suggests that they attempt to estimate how long the tasks will take. Figure 3-1 represents the approximate timetable that the four of them come up with. The meeting ends with each manager choosing to dis-

Figure 3-1 Timetable of tasks

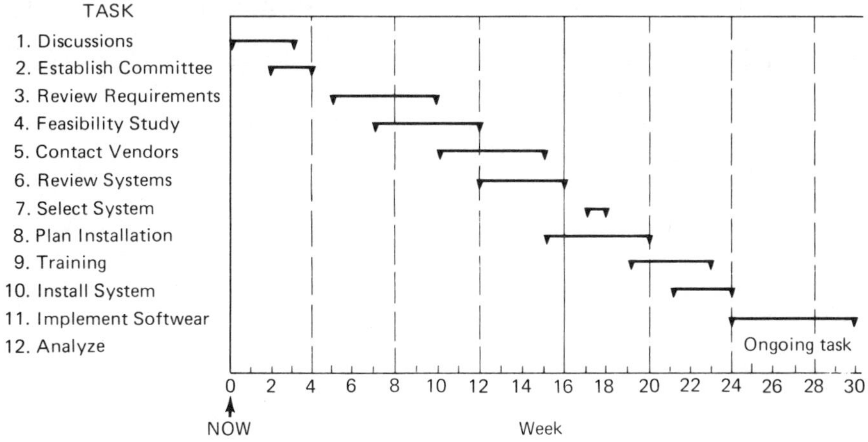

TASK

1. Discussions
2. Establish Committee
3. Review Requirements
4. Feasibility Study
5. Contact Vendors
6. Review Systems
7. Select System
8. Plan Installation
9. Training
10. Install System
11. Implement Softwear
12. Analyze

cuss the approach with their people during the next two days. John then calls a company-wide meeting for 3:00 P.M. on Friday. During the meeting, he discusses his ideas, answers questions, listens to both suggestions and fears. He assures the Stratford personnel that their ideas are welcomed. Mary forms the ad-hoc committee at the meeting as well, and each department elects one representative to that committee. Individual suggestions will be channeled through these representatives. John serves on the committee but in an ex-officio (nonvoting) capacity.

As the weeks roll along, the committee competently handles its various tasks. In the meantime, John authorizes the purchase of several $100 pocket computers so his people can get used to the new technology. The company also sets aside an additional $100 per person that can be used by each employee as he or she sees fit for their own education— books, night courses, seminars. Several employees take half a day and visit a noncompeting distribution business that's recently installed a company-wide computer system.

When the new computer is delivered twenty-four weeks after John's initial meeting with his three managers, everyone's prepared. Because of the planning and the involvement, the vendor of the $68,000 system is delighted at the smooth installation. Snags, blowups, and surprises were minimized and therefore the vendor realized a greater profit on the scale, making him much more willing to help John and his people.

The reason that I tell this brief tale is because it represents the exception rather than the rule. Tales of computer installations that have not gone smoothly far outnumber their counterparts.

To review:

1. People will fear a change if they believe that they will not be better off for it.
2. It takes an honest and healthy enthusiasm on the part of the manager or business owner to present people with enough information that they can understand the benefits of a particular change.
3. Computers can be more confounding to people because of a host of misconceptions about them.
4. Providing answers can clear up most of the confusion and head off problems long before they arise.

Issues for Managers

4

We are rapidly reaching a point at which every supervisor, manager, executive, and business owner will be affected one way or another by the computer. The information processor, a generic term for all sizes and types of data processors (computers) and word processors, will actually change the process of management and the way managers do their jobs. In many ways, computerization can be a powerful force for moving in the direction of more humanistic management. In my days of corporate management and business ownership in the 1960s and 1970s, I spent a great deal of time with numerical analysis, constantly scrutinizing quantities like gross margin, market share, and breakeven points. I also spent a lot of time chasing down data and information. In many ways, I was typical of what some people called the management scientist. I believed then, as many still believe today, that all problems could be solved by the use of quantitative analysis, methodology, and operations research techniques. Much of this worship of the science of management, which often ignored the art of management, was justified by that most insidious phrase, the bottom line. Because we focused on a measurable, calculable quantity, we forgot the impact of management changes on people. Pure management science dedicated to increased profit at any cost meant that General Electric, Westinghouse, and Allis-Chalmers could fix prices; United States Steel and other coal-mining companies could tear apart our countrysides with no responsibility for reclamation; Ford Motor Company could introduce an automobile with a known life-threatening defect; Hooker Chemical could dump not just toxic but lethal chemicals wherever they believed they had the right to do so. All this came from management science and a sole dedication to bottom-line performance.

We're now at a crossroads in management. We can continue to believe that more systems—be they new techniques or new machines—will miraculously cure our organizational diseases, or we can face the issue squarely that the answer lies in loving our fellow men and women and treating them with dignity. Computers should be looked on as machines to free us from the time we spend number-crunching so we can spend more time with our people. People solve problems, not computers. You will make your organization more healthy, viable, *and* profitable by focusing more on the people and less on the methodology. Use the computer and the word processor as tools, not masters; let them do the analyses. Spend your time with your people; fall in love with them, not some technology.

Management and Information

About 20 B.C. (before computers) managers often depended on subordinates for a great deal of the information needed for decision making. When I was with IBM, my boss often asked me to perform financial analyses of various asset investments—for example, a new building. I gathered data on costs and projected revenues, conducted the standard internal rate of return calculations, and presented my findings to him. He then decided whether or not to present the project to top management. This arrangement worked very well. I had an opportunity to learn and participate in important projects and he didn't have to do intricate analysis. Today, with VDTs everywhere, including the chief executive's office, things are much different. Modern managers can wind up in one of two positions—having too little information or having too much information. Let's look at each phenomenon separately.

Too Little Information

Not having enough information for effective decision making occurs as a result of:

1. Poorly designed computer systems in which programs, data bases, or both are constructed with little thought given to what is really wanted.
2. Reluctance on the part of the manager to gain computer literacy.

The first of these conditions is rectified by studying how data can be manipulated to give the kind of information managers can use to create desired results.

I was a marketing consultant to a medium-size precision metal manufacturing company that had twenty salespeople in the United States calling on existing and potential customers. The company's problem was how to help the sales force identify good prospects for new business. In a rather limited test, we asked two salesmen in different parts of the country to "smokestack,"—that is, to call on every industrial facility in their region they believed might be likely candidates for our products. The result? After two months, we had one $2,000 order. At that time, McGraw-Hill estimated a sales call cost an average of $68. If we assumed that each of our two salesmen made four calls per day, in a total of eighty man-days we blew about $20,000. There had to be a better way.

The company secured some new customers through advertising and promotion, and we wondered if it was possible to profile these in terms of size (number of employees or annual sales) and industry using the government's Standard Industrial Classification (SIC) code. When the plant received an inquiry (letter, phone call) from potential customers, each lead was passed on to the appropriate salesperson in the geographic sales region. Marketing personnel at headquarters then asked the salesperson to follow up on the leads and report what happened. Sometimes it was only a request for literature and other times an actual order resulted. If an order was placed by a new customer, was it possible to find our competitors for that order through SIC codes?

We purchased a file of some 30,000 manufacturing companies from Dun & Bradstreet, and when a customer placed his or her first order, we searched the file and listed every other business with that SIC. Next, we removed all current customers from that list and sorted the remaining companies by sales region. Periodically, each regional manager received a list of possible new customers for business development. This brief example illustrates what is meant by thinking through what you want and then working toward a solution. Information is cheap and readily available to all. The United States Government has massive amounts of data on population and business. Both profit and nonprofit private research organizations abound. Nearly any kind of data base can be uncovered if you're willing to spend the necessary time; but you must know what you want as an end result. First concentrate on the result you want, not the process or program you believe will get you to that result.

Reluctance to learn is a totally different kind of phenomenon. In some cases, our old friend fear raises its head, but many times a manager may feel he or she is simply too far removed from computer technology to ever understand it fully. Age is often a factor here. Roger Sullivan, the director of corporate education for the Commercial Union Insurance Company in Boston, divides his organization into three categories:

1. **Age group 20–30:** These people will probably move on from the company to other organizations and careers. They're very knowledgeable about computers, having seen them in college and even high school. They have no fear of the machines and their programs but do have a high need to move upward rapidly in terms of salary and position.
2. **Age group 30–40:** This group is anxious to get involved with computers. They've heard that computers are "in" and realize much of their advancement depends on computer literacy. They're open to new ideas and techniques and can generally be regarded as highly motivated to learn computerization.
3. **Age group 40 +:** People in this category tend to be more fearful of computers and may even be jealous of the ease with which younger managers and professionals move within electronic media.

If managers believe they'll not be able to learn the effective use of computers, they'll create experiences to support their beliefs. It's the self-fulfilling prophecy all over again. Therefore, the belief must change before the experience can manifest itself. Managers and others in the workforce can create a belief in computer competency from the standpoint that they have been successful in the past in learning new methods and procedures and can be just as successful with this new technology. The benefits of computer competency for today's manager directly relate to proficiency on the job. As time goes on, computer-illiterate managers will have a more difficult time finding and holding a job. If it takes motivation to change beliefs, the potential of being technically obsolete can provide that high level of motivation.

Too Much Information

Many managers are drowning in data but starving for real information, and poor systems design is a major factor. Because computers can handle a great deal of information in a short time, many people feel computers should regurgitate all this information in every possible way. Consequently, managers often receive high stacks of 132-column-wide paper, a lot of which goes home to start the family fireplace or wood stove. Another common effect is that the number of reports generated by the computer increases with time.

Kristina comes to work in the purchasing department of the Able Manufacturing Company. At the last place she worked, she received regular reports on suppliers who were more than one week late with promised deliveries. Working with her boss and the computer department, she institutes the same kind of report at Able. After two years, she leaves for another company, but the report continues. Steve replaces Kristina at Able and wants a deficiency report on vendors who don't supply goods and materials to Able's specifications. He gets his new report and the amount of processing time and paper increases again.

One company that I was with produced 126 monthly reports for 12 marketing and sales managers. The amount of paper completely filled the back seat of a car. One month I decided to hold back the reports just to see what would happen; less than half the managers called to find out where their reports were. When I polled everyone, I discovered that few of the reports were used. Some of this was traced to the fact that these managers didn't know what they were looking at; but the real issue was that these people were reluctant to come forward and say that many of the reports were not usable. Reports had been created over time and new ones added to the heap, but no one culled the useless ones. The 126 reports were reduced to 13, saving countless hours and dollars.

If your organization has become top heavy in reports of one kind or another, it may be time for a thorough analysis of just what is being produced and whether or not it's useful. Getting people to be honest about whether they really use a report may be a little difficult at first. Some people may be afraid to admit they find some reports irrelevant. They may feel making such a confession will make them look dumb (that the manager will say, "Why didn't you say so before this?"), or they might figure their status somehow depends on the number and frequency of reports they receive. If such an analysis is approached openly with an emphasis toward streamlining and winnowing the chaff, the negative effects will be lessened.

Let's discuss another effect of managers having too much information. With VDTs multiplying like rabbits in our organizations, managers and executives now have direct access to information they never had before. In past years, if an executive wanted information for decision making, he or she often delegated that task to a subordinate and waited several days or even weeks for the data to be gathered, analyzed, and presented. Now, many managers need only a terminal and some computer savvy to get information in minutes that used to take days.

I'm certainly not against even chief executives having information more rapidly. Good information contributes to good decision making, and one of the parameters of "good" information is its timeliness. There can be some problems with this approach, however, as Mary Bralove wrote in an article for the January 12, 1983, *Wall Street Journal* entitled "Direct Data: Some Chief Executives Bypass, and Irk, Staffs in Getting Information." Some of the major points of her article were:

1. Many managers, frustrated waiting for month-end reports that are ancient history by the time they are received, have learned to access data bases on their own.

2. Staff people, who previously saw themselves as an integral part of the information power base, may perceive they are losing power and status by being bypassed.

3. Managers who become enthralled with what a VDT can do for them may lose sight of "less tangible matters such as grooming executives."

4. If a chief executive with a talent for using information systems isn't careful, he or she may be seen as a meddler. It can be extremely embarrassing to a subordinate to be confronted by the boss with an I-have-this-information–why-don't-you approach.

I think the issues discussed in Ms. Bralove's article are clear. Managers need to approach information-gathering with care. Special attention should be given to any attempts to use the computer for individual or departmental performance monitoring. People don't like to be spied on; to them it often means they're not trusted. Treat people as if they're not trusted and they'll begin to behave in an untrustworthy manner. You get what you concentrate on.

Using information systems to promote management by surprise doesn't work either. Some managers believe that surprises keep people on their toes; more likely, it keeps them on their backs. It takes great skill and caring to handle some piece of information that others may have overlooked. Your discovery should not be used as a weapon against others but merely as a part of an overall effort to improve conditions. Share the information, but do it as a team member, not an autocrat.

Coming Changes in Management

It shouldn't be a surprise to anyone in management that vast changes are occurring and even greater ones will occur in the near future. Managers across the world now stand at a very critical crossroad, a crossroad that's more imaginary than real. Imagine you're at a mythical fork in a road. The left fork is labeled "Systems and Technology" and the right path "Human Development." Some people see a division in a road as offering only one of two choices—the left or the right. There is a third choice: the choice to take *both paths simultaneously.* More and more managers today are becoming aware that human beings are the most valuable asset of an organization. Take people out of business or non-profit organizations and all you have are buildings, land, machinery, and fixtures. However, to deny we're a technological society is to deny present reality. The successful manager in the years to come must have a dual focus, keeping one eye on people and the other on information processing.

Probably one of the biggest changes already underway is the reduced ranks of middle manager, that person who sits in the corporate hierarchy somewhere between top managers (the CEO and subordinate executives) and first-line supervisors. A great deal of the winnowing occurs as a direct result of the computer and, although estimates vary, the reduction may eventually be as high as 50 percent of present levels by the end of the 1980s. The British writer David Clutterbuck ("The Whittling Away of Middle Management," *International Management,* copyright 1982, McGraw-Hill Publications Co.) sees four factors responsible for this change:

1. Swollen middle-management ranks resulting largely from inaccurate predictions over the past twenty years.
2. A general demand for higher productivity that places more emphasis on automated machinery and robots. According to David Birch at MIT, the number of employees engaged in manufacturing declined 4 percent, from 19,800,000 to 19,000,000, between 1970 and 1976. As we automate our offices and service organizations in the 1980s, we can expect the same thing to happen. Less people to supervise means fewer managers.
3. As more higher-echelon managers have access to computer-prepared analyses, the need for middle-level staff personnel will decline.
4. Organizations are not only becoming "flatter" (fewer intermediate levels), they're focusing more on their core businesses and less on running widely diversified conglomerates.

I don't believe that we'll see the unemployment lines swollen with MBAs. The thinning process will take place gradually and displaced managers will find other things to do, including getting into consulting or their own businesses. The point is, there will be fewer middle managers in the future. Managers of the future who do survive and flourish will need to be highly computer literate and humanists as well.

One other effect contributing to a lessening of the number of managers is a tendency toward a larger span of control or the number of people supervised. In the 1930s, a typical span of control was forty people, but by the 1960s the average span of control had dropped to seven individuals. With a growing emphasis on cohesive, integrated work groups, the need for close supervision diminishes. Although the span of control will probably increase in the 1980s, managers will "boss" less and communicate more, especially as they learn that nearly everyone performs superbly if treated humanely and with dignity.

Management is also becoming more decentralized. The net effect is that more decision making occurs at lower levels in the organization. Because subordinate managers and staff people have access to more information with computerization, it makes sense to move the decision-making process down the organizational hierarchy. This also means that top-level managers must delegate more of their power, and some executives do not want to do so. Their reasons vary but usually include one or more of the following beliefs:

1. My subordinates lack the proper experience.
2. It takes more time to explain than to do.
3. Their mistakes could be very costly.
4. I can get action more quickly.
5. There are things I should do myself.
6. My people don't have the knowledge.

7. My people are already too busy.
8. They aren't ready for more responsibility.
9. I will lose control of the situation.
10. I make better decisions.

Obviously, in some cases, especially with young men and women brand new to the workforce, a few of these beliefs may be valid, but in many cases the beliefs are merely excuses stemming from a fear of losing power and status. Let's couch delegation in terms of love and wisdom; if we give away love and wisdom, we wind up with more than we started with. The way to receive love and wisdom is to give it away constantly. Sow the wind and reap the whirlwind. There's a catch to all this, though: You can't give away what you don't have. You can't sell love or wisdom short. You must first love yourself fully and see yourself as someone possessing wisdom.

The secret of delegation lies with you. You must do it. In a handout that I use in my management training seminars, I stress what I call the YOU factor in delegation:

1. YOU tend to delegate more tasks as you gain experience, setting broader limits with your subordinates.
2. YOU assign complicated tasks in bits and pieces.
3. YOU never make totally complete assignments; give your subordinates "open" areas to use their creativity.
4. YOU always take the ultimate responsibility for jobs that you delegate and YOU may have to accept all the blame and none of the praise.
5. YOU must review what you've assigned and YOU must alter your behavior as a function of this feedback. YOU must inspect what YOU expect.
6. YOU set the limits on a subordinate's authority.
7. YOU determine your subordinate's commitment or the lack of it.
8. YOU provide the positive expectations.
9. YOU judge the performance.
10. YOU continue the process and build success for yourself and for others.

One Final Note on Coming Changes

It's my personal feeling that the science of management has been overemphasized in the 1960s and 1970s and, as a result, we're still faced with many of the problems in our organizations that have plagued us for decades—absenteeism, turnover, grievances, low morale, inefficiency. I'm not suggesting that we throw out some of the good techniques that we've developed, but that we balance the science of management with the art of management and the personal style of each individual manager. Management science, like the other sciences (biology, chemistry, physics), tries to reduce some phenomenon to a uniform set of repeatable and predictable rules. If you are performing an investment analysis, for example, you might use the prescribed format of discounted cash flow and internal rate of return analysis. That's as it should be, but management science has little to say about intuitive judgments and the use of feeling and emotion—more a part of the art of management than the science. The other problem that management science precipitates is a loss of individual style. As I have stressed before, no two people are alike, and organizations that have fostered groupthink have lost the creativity that comes from personalized thinking and action. We should work toward an integration of science, art, and style in the 1980s that will serve to balance our decision making and make people more effective as well as more satisfied.

Issues Involving Workers

5

Let's talk a little bit about what workers like and don't like about work. First of all, what do workers want? I'm not going to review the answers of the four giants in management theory—Abraham Maslow, Douglas McGregor, David McClelland, and Frederick Herzberg—but I urge you to read what they say, and any good general management text will give you the basics.

In *Effective Management—A Humanistic Perspective*, Joseph P. Cangemi and George E. Guttschalk (New York: Philosophical Library, 1980) discuss a survey of 35,000 workers and their supervisors: The employees rated ten things they wanted from their work and their organizations. The top three, in order, were

1. Full appreciation for work done
2. Feeling "in" on things
3. Sympathetic understanding of personal problems

When the supervisors' rankings were totalled, they rated those same three in order of importance right at the bottom of the list—numbers 8, 10, and 9, respectively. What supervisors thought was the most important item, good wages, had been placed fifth by the workers, halfway down the list. Essentially, the employees wanted to feel loved but the supervisors didn't see things that way. They thought they could do it with money. But money doesn't equal love. I'm not saying money isn't important; it's just not as important as some people believe. The other point is that if you, as a supervisor, manager, or executive, believe your people want one thing (money) when they actually want something else (love), you're going to have a rough time. You'll put your efforts toward getting greater efficiency but those efforts won't work. If you're not careful, you can even lose your faith in people because you believe you're not appreciated.

There are lots of worker surveys; there are also manager surveys. A common thread between the two is that neither likes abstractions. They like people. They'll put up with abstractions—graphs, filling out forms, formulas, computers—but not if there's little or no human contact. A number of years ago, I came up with an acronym for remembering what people—hourly workers, first-line supervisors, top executives—want from their jobs. The word I use is GRAPES, and it works out like this:

Growth
Recognition
Achievement
Participation
Expectation
Sensitivity

Growth means learning new skills and in general expanding one's base of wisdom. Wisdom can be thought of as the highest level of a hierarchy.

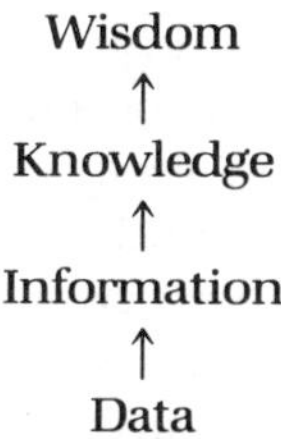

We begin with data that is operated on somehow (by a person or a computer) to give information that acts as a base for decision making. When we assemble enough information to truly understand a situation, we possess knowledge; we know and know we know. Wisdom, it is said, is knowledge with caring and love. Recognition is something everyone needs. Without recognition by another human being, we have no way of knowing how we're doing. Workers strive so hard for recognition that they may even produce negative behavior such as absenteeism to gain it. We are all achievers to one degree or another. Most people enjoy setting goals for themselves and then moving toward the accomplishment of those goals. This is the basic idea behind MBO (management by objectives); but unfortunately many organizations attach negative connotations to *not* reaching goals. It's far better to analyze why an objective wasn't attained than berate someone for not doing so. Participation is closely linked to Maslow's affiliation; people like to work with other people. A human being can't exist alone. In a world of over four billion people, no one can cite a case of a solitary human. People may choose to live alone or even be reclusive, but they need some form of contact. The worst fate for a prisoner is solitary confinement, yet many of our modern offices seem to be creating their own version of this direst of punishments. Expectation refers to the positive feeling managers and subordinates have about how work will turn out. If you expect quality from yourself and others, the chances are you'll get it. It's really a self-fulfilling prophecy; you get what you concentrate on. If you, as a manager, believe that people are lazy, that's exactly what you'll get because you treat them that way. If, on the other hand, you focus on the dignity of the human spirit in all people, the results you see will be positive and rewarding. Sensitivity means an awareness of what people want and, when possible, giving it to them. One definition of love is that you want the same things for those you deeply care about as they want for themselves. Sometimes you simply can't give someone what they want because it's impossible, like tripling someone's salary. You don't need to feel guilty about that and you can still want it for them. Sensitivity means going beyond just the situations at work. Contrary to some leftover beliefs, people can't leave their personal problems at home. People are total beings; they can't compartmentalize. If Steve is having a rough separation and divorce, or Joan's mother has terminal cancer, of course they'll be distraught, upset, and nervous, and it will affect their work. Sometimes just being there with an understanding ear helps greatly.

The whole GRAPES theory really comes down to the two factors I've stressed all along—wisdom and love. You must first possess them yourself before you can give them away. You must know yourself and you must love yourself. As Leo Buscaglia so often asks, "How can you give something away you don't have to begin with?"

Organizations themselves operate under one of the four basic assumptions shown in Figure 5-1. Unless you and your organization operate under the principles of wisdom and love, your attempts to bring about a technical change like computerization will be much more difficult than it has to be.

Now let's address the subject of people and computers. First, let's discuss some research conducted in the early 1980s that's still applicable today.

Working Women, a national association of office workers, polled women employees who work with computers and word processors. The

Figure 5-1   Organizational assumptions

Wisdom but No Love
A rather cold and mechanistic organization that may grow but without human feeling.

Wisdom and Love
A living, breathing, and vitally functioning organization that is highly satisfying to its people and other "stakeholders"—customers, clients, suppliers, investors, the community.

No Wisdom, No Love
An organization plagued with ill will, low morale, absenteeism, turnover, insubordination, and totally lacking in both productivity and a sense of belonging.

Love but No Wisdom
Pure warmth and a sense of personal belonging but lacking aggressiveness to accomplish goals and objectives. More of a commune than a business.

association asked what these women like and what they don't like about their work. The results are no surprise. They like

- Social contacts with others
- Variety in their work
- Opportunities to advance
- Acquiring new skills
- Learning about their company and its industry

It looks like a variety of love-wisdom, doesn't it? They said they dislike

- A lack of respect from their supervisors
- The prospect of no advancement
- Low pay

Looking at the first two, you can say that the first represents no love and the second no wisdom—but how about the last one, low pay? What is the situation when people feel they aren't paid enough for what they do? It has nothing to do with meeting their bills. It has to do with recognition. When you give someone a raise, you recognize them. It means you care for them. In the words some religions use to describe their sacraments, it's an "outward and visible sign of an inward and spiritual grace." If you simply hand out raises because it's organizational policy, you're guilty of what lawyers call form over substance. The form (raise) is there, but it has no substance (love and concern).

Further data gathered in the study cites specific complaints about computerization. People working with VDTs see their work becoming more fragmented. Rather than working with a whole task from start to finish, each employee now sees only a part of a job. Although the study doesn't point this out specifically, any time work is fractionated, productivity and morale suffer. Most people like to work on a job from start to finish; and they like to work as part of a team where they can see the importance of what they're doing. They also enjoy planning how to do their work.

The parallel in the auto industry is clear. A number of years ago, Saab and Volvo changed their methods of manufacturing from an assembly line to having teams build an entire car. As might be expected, worker satisfaction increased as did quality. Costs did increase initially and prices had to be raised, but the move didn't harm car sales for these companies.

Dividing work into smaller and smaller subtasks may seem more efficient and, from a purely scientific standpoint, it may be so; people perform work, not machines. People have feelings, something that scientific management doesn't address. People feel that when they're only performing some small part of a larger job, their career paths are blocked, limiting their advancement and stifling them. The study by Working Women also found that although many of the employees surveyed admit computers and word processors allow them to increase their productivity, their organizations don't reward them for this efficiency in terms of higher pay. Their increased productivity resulted in decreased costs and higher profits for their companies, but they did not share in this reward, thus furthering any present "them-us" feeling.

Overall, the people surveyed don't see automation as benefitting them at all; they actually see it as *worsening* their work situation. As a result of computers, the employees found that they have

- Less variety in their work
- Fewer social contacts
- Lower relative pay
- More dull, boring, and routine jobs

Someone once defined marketing as: You find out what people want and give them more of it; you find out what they don't want and give them none of it. It seems to me that such a concise definition holds just as well for people in the workplace. If people want more variety, give it to them. Let them select their own work among themselves. If people want more social contacts, don't isolate them. If your organization is experiencing cost savings because of automation, pass those savings along to the very people who are making it possible.

Shoshanah Zuboff at MIT's Sloan School of Management also discovered similar negative factors associated with computer equipment. Some employers believe their people feel more professional about their jobs if they're given VDTs, but it doesn't happen. Again people complained about isolation and fewer social contacts. In addition, workers become disenfranchised with their work as a whole. They feel less satisfied with what they're doing because it's hard to measure what you're doing if you sit in front of a screen all day long. A pile of paper looks like work; a screen full of numbers doesn't. The former seems real and measurable, whereas the latter is too abstract.

Zuboff also found that people become more frustrated and angry with VDTs than they do with people. This comes as no surprise, because computers allow little room for negotiation. You can't sit and argue with a VDT. In so many cases I see, companies give almost no thought to the human factors connected with computers. In those cases, both the company and the computer are seen in a negative light by employees. People like to be creative and inventive. Most computer programs leave little room for personal creativity on the part of the operator. People using VDTs are stuck with a do-it-my-way-or-else situation, with the computer issuing the orders. Most individuals don't like to be ordered about by other people (an exception being emergency or life-and-death situations); imagine how they feel about being ordered by a machine.

People see the computer as removing not only their creativity but much of their decision-making power as well. I'm not against having computers do the routine, repetitive jobs people don't enjoy doing—for example, having a word processor justify (align) margins on the right-hand side of a page as you see in this book—but when individual judgment is lost, people feel like machines themselves. If a computer is using its own set of automated decision rules and the people are only feeding it data, the people feel like less than the machine, slaves to it. That's certainly not a way to create an energetic, satisfied, productive workforce.

A human being has the ability to hold two opposing views. A computer cannot. A computer, because of the way it works internally, examines options, but it must choose one of those options through a cold, mathematical process. There is no humanity present. Take the well-publicized case of a person playing chess against a human opponent versus a computer. In the case of human playing human, a vast amount of psychology comes into the picture: the amount of time elapsing between moves, eye contact, nervous gestures, sweating or the lack of it. A computer doesn't bite its nails or chain-smoke cigarettes; it simply sits there and issues commands.

To the worker, then, the computer is the worst kind of supervisor. It issues orders that must be followed. If those orders are not followed, the work doesn't get done. If the work doesn't get done, people feel that their jobs may be in jeopardy. Couple this with computer systems that monitor an employee's productivity (or the lack of it), and we have a procedure leading to resentment of management and the organization as a whole.

What are the solutions to these problems? Let's start with job design as a whole and what managers can do to make work more rewarding and pleasant while increasing productivity and decreasing errors and cost.

Reduce Close Supervision

If you look at photographs of people at work fifty years ago, you often see groups of men and women performing some task—running machines, assembling parts, typing letters—with a supervisor watching closely, fulfilling a role of overseer or taskmaster rather than that of manager. Time changed the need for that, if indeed the need ever existed. People don't like supervisors hanging over them. Most people actually like being physically removed from their bosses. One common error I see is a large room filled with people at desks whose supervisor sits in his or her office facing the group while looking out a glass window. People want their supervisors to be available to them to answer questions and for general consulting, but they don't want a watchman. Some organizations have tried a system of rotating supervisors. The military has used this system for years, and although armed forces management has its own special breed of problems, one of them isn't the regular turnover in commanding officers and NCO's.

Essentially what we're working toward is a more egalitarian workforce. People want more freedom, more autonomy and more decision making, with their supervisors acting more in the sense of true leaders. I often make the parallel between a supervisor and the conductor of a symphony orchestra. When you attend a symphony or watch one on television, you see the conductor setting the entire theme of the music—emphasis, timing, volume, participation by the musicians. What you don't see is the hours of rehearsal that precede the performance, rehearsals in which the conductor *interprets* the music of the composer. The conductor acts as a catalyst. The performance can't be carried out without the conductor, even though that person produces no music of his or her own.

Many managers feel their subordinates are little children needing constant supervision lest they stray from the straight and narrow. Like the devoted parent, they love their "children"; but they also labor under the false assumption that, left to their own devices, their charges will get into trouble. By and large, though, subordinates can direct their own efforts. They need and want guidance and attention, but that varies from individual to individual; and as subordinates gain in confidence, experience, and autonomy, they need less supervision. They want and need a manager for overall direction for their own growth and the awareness that their work is proper and important.

Provide More Information

It's been said that the biggest single problem in organizations is communication, and that normally means not enough of it. People want to and

should be informed about things affecting them. People want to know.
How do you feel when you don't know what's going on, how you're
doing, what's expected, or how you fit in? Managers can provide information in four ways:

Identify
Delegate
Explain
Signify

The're easy to remember because the letters spell IDES.

1. Identify   People's jobs need identity just as people need identity.
We hear the term *identity crisis*; some people have a job identity crisis—
they want to see how their job fits into the whole. They want an identifi-
able job with a visible outcome.

2. Delegate   Most people want more responsibility, and any manager can do this by giving away work. Too many managers spend too
much time doing tasks that their people can do, enjoy doing, and *might*
do better. Managers have lots of excuses why they don't delegate more:
Their people are too busy (the people should be asked); the manager
does it more quickly (probably, but people need to grow, and besides, if
the task is routine, a manager can give it away and concentrate on the
creative); the manager has the authority (the employee can be given the
authority or the manager can let the employee do the work but retain
the final authority). Employees need to know the limits of their authority and what is expected of them. They need guidance and to be told
how they're doing. They need explanations.

3. Explain   People need feedback both from peers and from their
bosses. One of the best ways to accomplish this is by mutual goal setting.
Let's say a manager and a subordinate decide the subordinate will work
toward new goals—reducing the time to perform certain tasks, learning
a new skill, decreasing the number of errors. As the employee makes
progress toward each of these, the manager gives advice, guidance, and
other feedback. Compare this with the institution of MBO where subordinates are often negatively criticized when goals are not reached,
thereby teaching employees that setting objectives only gets them in
trouble. Managers and subordinates should analyze why a goal isn't met,
but finger-pointing and blame only weaken the process. Managers need
to explain organizational policies and procedures so people know
what's happening and what's expected of them. Supervisors must realize
people want to do a variety of tasks, and this is especially true in the
computerized office. Managers explain the overall approach, but employees work out the routine.

If supervisors constantly evaluate people, maybe we can do away with the deadly annual employee rating system.

4. Signify By this word, I mean managers provide information as to the importance (significance) of the tasks employees perform. Take the example used earlier of an insurance clerk using a VDT to process claims. It's vital to signify that the job is not simply entering proper numbers into the computer, but that there is a human being out there who needs to be helped. People want to perform meaningful work that has a positive impact on other people, either inside or outside the organization.

The Positive Impact of Information Systems

It may seem as if I'm saying that the quality of life in our automated organizations is destined to decline. I'm not, but I am pointing to potential areas of difficulty that can remove people from contact with others, decrease the importance of their jobs, and diminish the variety in their work. However, information systems can be of tremendous benefit to both people as individuals and the organization as a whole. How can this be accomplished?

1. The installation of a computer system presents an opportunity to reorganize decision making and communication on a group-centered basis rather than a supervisor-centered one. Groups can
   a. Assign tasks and schedule work
   b. Set group and individual goals
   c. Evaluate group and individual performance
   d. Determine rewards and punishments
   e. Monitor progress and report on it to management
   f. Handle problems
   g. Plan
2. A computer system creates new job skills requiring new knowledge. Usually this leads to greater job satisfaction and higher pay as well.
3. Communications can be improved by using the computer system for electronic and voice mail, word processing, computer phone message systems, teleconferencing, and the like.
4. On-the-job annoyances such as searching for information and retyping documents can be reduced.
5. People go through technological changes that enhance future changes.

What I'm saying is that computerization presents just the right "excuse" for making positive changes in the workplace. If employees are allowed more control over what's happening; if they're given more planning and decision-making responsibility; if managers are free to do more training and give more personal attention to workers; if more career opportunities open up—then quality, interaction, and efficiency increase; costs, turnover, and dissatisfaction decrease.

For these changes to occur properly, management must:

- Give its total support to the changes
- Assure people they'll benefit from the computer and not lose their jobs
- Have confidence in themselves so they can have confidence in workers
- Be prepared to support education and training for all people who will work with automation

Because the last element is so important to the overall success of computer systems, we'll devote the next chapter to the subject of training.

Training

6

Do organizations really save time and money when they provide little or no training? That must be the prevailing belief, because it happens every day. When businesses experience a downturn in sales and profits, training is often one of the first things cut from the budget. Evidently many managers feel people's needs to grow and learn on their jobs somehow relates to business conditions. Even in profitable times, top managers are often reluctant to invest in training because they have difficulty calculating the return on that investment.

If a manufacturing company is considering a $100,000 machine or tool, a financial analysis showing cost savings, the payback period, and the percent annual rate of return is often performed. It's a relatively straightforward calculation that most business administration graduates can do. However, because the same calculations for an investment in training aren't so easy to perform, they're rarely done. Actually, there are two ways to do such an analysis. The first way uses the overall cost justification of the *entire* automation process. In this approach, the cost of training is included with all other costs: hardware, software, maintenance, supplies. The total costs are then compared to the cost savings produced by increased effectiveness and efficiency. Effectiveness means the ability to do *useful* tasks that can't be performed without processing equipment, whereas efficiency refers to a faster, more accurate way of doing a task. An example of increased effectiveness is a computer in a medical practice (physician, dentist, veterinarian) programmed to send reminder cards automatically to patients regarding such things as annual physicals, periodic dental examinations and cleaning, or immunizations for the family pet. Replacing a typewriter with a word processor for letter and report preparation is an example of increased efficiency.

Cost justification and financial analysis of training can also be performed on an individual basis. To do this we need an estimate of the increase in effectiveness and efficiency that can be expected as a result of training. Such estimates are usually available from those who will be doing the training.

Let's look at a clerical employee whose total cost to the company is $10 per hour and assume that a one-week training course will improve the output of that person by 20 percent. The course, including expenses, costs $1200 and the company will lose the services of that person for one week, which represents another $400, bringing the total cost to $1600. Now, a 20 percent improvement is like getting one more workday per week or $80 (8 hours times $10) in savings. Thus, the training will pay for itself in

$$\frac{\$1600}{\$80} = 20 \text{ weeks}$$

The Need for Training

Many managers make two basic errors when they consider training in information processing and automation: They focus only on the issue of efficiency, and they assume only equipment operators need training.

When a business acquires word-processing equipment, management generally feels that typists, secretaries, clerks, and other administrative workers should receive keyboard training only until they learn to type faster and more accurately. This is like teaching someone to drive a car without ever explaining what the gauges on the dashboard mean. While it's certainly true that novice drivers don't have to know the theory of the Sterling heat cycle, they do need basic knowledge of the automobile so they don't *create* problems and are able to recognize them if they occur before something like overheating destroys the engine. There was an older woman in our neighborhood who purchased her first car, which ran erratically after it had warmed up. No one could find the problem until a local mechanic asked the lady to take him for a drive. He recognized the problem immediately; the woman would pull out the manual choke lever and use it as a hanger for her pocketbook. Similarly, people have "crashed" computer systems because they didn't know what they were doing.

I believe it's important to give full training to operators, including theory of operation, overall capabilities, specific tasks, error messages, potential problems, operator-level maintenance, and expansion possibilities. With this more expansive training, operators feel more comfortable with the equipment and are more capable of making suggestions for increasing the effectiveness of the system.

Consider the following fictional story about a Maine lumberjack who wanted to increase the amount of timber he cut. He visited a local power equipment dealer who convinced him he could cut five times as much timber if he bought a chain saw to replace his manual bucksaw. A month later, the lumberjack returned complaining that instead of increasing the number of trees, his productivity was only one fourth of what it was with his handsaw. The dealer looked the saw over, pulled the starter cord, and the saw roared to life. The lumberjack looked very perplexed and asked, "What's that noise?"

Not only do operators require instruction, managers themselves often need training about information-processing systems. Certainly the training requirements for a top executive differ from those for a first-line supervisor, but the need is there nonetheless. Managers need hands-on experience with the equipment so they can appreciate what their people are dealing with and empathize with them when problems occur. They also must know the capabilities and limitations of the systems so they don't request something that can't be done. At a small college where I taught, the registrar would make outlandish demands on the data-processing department because she never took the time to learn what the computer could and could not do. A great deal of time was wasted, tempers flared, and interdepartmental relations deteriorated because of this lack of knowledge.

Overall Approach to Training

In *Office Automation: A Manager's Guide for Improved Productivity* (New York: John Wiley & Sons, 1982) Lieberman, Selig, and Walsh suggest a three-phase approach to training:

1. Preinstallation training explains the basic concepts of the equipment. The planning schedule for overall implementation is covered in this phase so that all are aware of when the changeover will occur. Questions are answered and fears allayed. The basic purpose of preinstallation training is to head off problems after the equipment is in use.
2. Installation training occurs while the equipment is being readied to be brought into full use.
3. Post-installation training handles the issue of further effectiveness of the equipment. The major purpose of this phase, however, is to answer group and individual questions and to support those intimately connected with the information processing.

This overall approach to training should be discussed with the equipment vendor for two major reasons. In the first place, the timing of the training in relation to installation is important. If preinstallation training is done, the equipment should be brought in shortly after this first phase is complete. Second, most vendors provide training as a part of the total cost of the system. The training they provide may not be as complete as you want; for example, few vendors provide much theory and concept training. You'll want to coordinate the training efforts, especially if different phases are handled by different techniques or teachers.

In addition to timing of training so it revolves around the installation of the equipment, consider your audience. We can break that audience into three groups: executives, supervisors, and users. The needs of these people differ as a function of their overall responsibilities regarding automation. Top executives or business owners typically focus on long-range goals and are concerned with growth and profits. This group, the smallest in number of the three categories, needs to see how the expenditure for the equipment, training, software, maintenance, and supplies is a beneficial move for the organization. It's critical that higher-level managers recognize the impact of automation on *all* levels. All too often executives pay little attention to the impact of their decisions on the people who must implement them. There is a tendency to regard automation as just another business decision made in the name of efficiency. If an organization spends $50,000 or $500,000 on a program to use information processing, the executives of that organization can rightfully expect a return on that investment in the form of increased revenue, decreased costs, and an expanded capability—more tasks accomplished in the same amount of time. If, after some period of time following the installation of the equipment, these benefits are not realized, executives may be quick to blame their subordinate managers for failing to produce the expected returns. This process can quickly degrade into the mother-spanks-child, child-kicks-dog, dog-bites-cat process of negative displacement. Top executives must recognize that if an automation program fails to reach its stated goals, it does little good to start spreading blame; the chances are that improper or insufficient training is the real culprit.

Supervisors, especially first-line supervisors of the equipment users, need more training than top executives. They need to know how their departments and people will be affected and how automation will affect their supervisory role. For instance, if operators are expected to perform a majority of their tasks using a VDT, supervisors must be aware of some of the factors that I spoke about earlier—boredom, frustration, fear, loneliness. They must realize that although automation can be fun, rewarding, and challenging, it also can bring its own very special brand of problems. The important point is not to dwell on the problems but rather on ways to circumvent them before they arise.

By far, equipment users need the most training. They need assurances: (1) that their skills won't be downgraded, and (2) that they won't lose their jobs. This is a supervisory responsibility but still part and parcel of the user's training. The users should be given education in the basic principles of information processing. I don't think it's necessary to spend days going over the theory of operation of the central processing unit, but the basic terminology should be covered as well as the benefits to the employee and to the organization. Some of this early training may be done without equipment. After the users grasp the concepts, they can move into hands-on training with the actual equipment itself. Most organizations prefer doing this part of the training off-site and before the equipment installation.

The next phase takes place after installation. Sometimes all that's required, if the earlier training is complete, is that knowledgeable people be available to the operators to answer questions and provide help when needed. The post-installation phase of training may consist of nothing more than holding discussion groups among the users to determine what problems they're having and how the problems may be resolved.

Types and Sources of Training

1. Vendors Nearly every purveyor of computer and word-processing equipment provides some level of training, but usually only for operators. However, they're often excellent sources of information about training for executives and supervisors and extended training for users. Usually vendor training occurs at a branch office, local dealership, or vendor headquarters. These classes may vary in length from one day to two weeks, with the average being five days. The vendor may also conduct some training at the customer's location. The number of people trained as a part of the equipment purchase also may vary; the industry norm seems to be one operator trained per machine purchased. Some vendors depend on self-instructional, self-paced multimedia packages or computer-aided instruction (CAI), which we'll discuss shortly. However, few vendors provide much post-installation instruction and discussion.

2. Commercial Schools There are a large number of private, profit-making schools offering instruction in data and word processing. Although many of these schools cater to individuals acting on their own behalf to further their skills, some of these institutions are geared to help organizations with their overall training needs. And although there are many reputable schools, including some run on a national basis by large corporations, there are some fly-by-nighters lured into the market by the phenomenal growth in the computer industry and the opportu-

72

nity to turn a fast profit with little investment. Be sure to investigate past performance thoroughly before using any training organization.

3. **Colleges and Universities**   Many of the nation's institutions of higher learning are involved in computer training. Most often, these schools offer college-credit courses meeting eight to sixteen weeks for a total of forty hours of instruction. Some colleges also offer other approaches such as mini-courses that may meet on Saturdays or all-day seminars. A call to the director of continuing education will tell you what's available and the cost.

One problem with the outside course approach is that classes often meet after normal working hours—evenings and weekends. This can be a ticklish situation. Should management *require* employees to give up some of their free time? I don't think so, because it can easily lead to bitterness and resentment; as with all training, the trainees should be consulted.

4. **Consultants**   There are lots of private consultants and consulting or training firms that specialize in this area. College professors also may do some of this after hours. Unlike vendors, the training that consultants provide is usually independent of any equipment being acquired. However, these folks may be excellent sources for the managerial part of the training.

5. **Seminars and Conferences**   There are many seminars and conferences offered around the country on all phases of automation. Some of these are run by large organizations, such as the American Management Association (AMA). However, some consider the cost of AMA seminars disproportionately high compared to the quality of instruction. Many of the Computer Science Departments in the nation's larger universities sponsor one- to three-day seminars on their campuses. In addition, professional organizations, industry groups, and trade associations run conferences on automation. Again, these sessions are more for managers than operators.

6. **Nonhuman Instruction**   There are two types of self-learning techniques that often appeal to users. The first is called programmed instruction (PI), which uses a teaching manual and workbook in which the student records his or her progress. Sometimes a series of audio cassettes accompanies the printed material. PI, being self-paced, is often an excellent and inexpensive way to learn some of the basics of data and word processing before training on the equipment takes place.

The second type of individual training is called computer-aided instruction, or CAI. This form of instruction uses the computer itself as a teacher. This type of training is normally for operators, and the computer or word processor leads the students through exercises while they're at the keyboard. Operators are allowed (sometimes even made) to make mistakes and to learn from them in a practice environment before confronting the real thing. Sometimes two people can work together using a buddy system for learning.

CAI packages, often contained on floppy disks, are used by many vendors but should not replace human training. The CAI only can answer questions that fit into the instructional program; this is too limiting. In addition, some CAI packages aren't very user-friendly and may be more intimidating than instructional.

In-House, Out-of-House

A question often arises regarding the benefits and disadvantages of on-premise (in-house) versus off-premise (out-of-house) training. I think there should be both. It is probably best to train executives and supervisors in a location outside of the company. There are many reasons for this, but one of the most important is to remove the temptation to run back to the office at breaks or lunch. This training is important to them and to the organization as a whole, and it should not be interrupted by changes in focus.

When training is provided at the vendor's location, office and clerical personnel (the users) are also given the opportunity to get away from their desks and their phones for a few days.

Training at the time of installation will certainly be conducted in-house. Since VDTs can be moved around an organization relatively easily, it's a good idea to conduct some group training with everyone in one place before operators begin using the equipment at their desks. The site for group training should have the same general lighting and decor as the work areas. Enough time should be allotted for the training to take place; the process must not be rushed. Although CAI can be used for some of this group training, there should be someone available for instruction and to answer individual questions. Again, the user buddy system seems to work well as long as it's not totally unstructured.

Mark Johnson and Jim Murchison, writing in the February 1982 issue of *Datamation* ("In-House DP Training"), describe an approach taken by Blue Cross/Blue Shield of North Carolina for user-level training. First, notices were posted stating that the company wanted to provide this type of training. Administrative and clerical personnel who showed an interest were interviewed regarding their needs for their jobs and what they wanted to learn. During these sessions, two important points were stressed. In the first place, no one would be forced to go and there would be no black marks on a person's record if they chose not to attend. Second, no promises were made regarding promotions or salary increases for those who took the training.

Based on the need survey, Blue Cross/Blue Shield approached a nearby university for a tailor-made course that addressed the special needs of their poeple. They found this particular approach gave three additional benefits: The cost to BC/BS was less than alternate approaches; the professor was able to give more personal attention to the students; the professor had student conference hours for one-on-one discussions for individuals requiring more help.

The course was held after working hours, two nights a week, three hours per night, for sixteen weeks. At the request of a majority of the students, the course stressed business applications of information processors. Of the thirty individuals who began the course, twenty-eight completed it and for their ninety-six hours of instruction they received 9.6 continuing education units or CEUs, the equivalent of two undergraduate courses.

Let's go through a training plan for a small manufacturing company.

A Training Scenario

The Norwich Company sells outdoor, sports, and hiking equipment in their five retail stores located in the Midwest. However, the majority of Norwich's business consists of orders received by mail as a result of their nationally distributed catalog. There are over one hundred people working in the catalog sales division, many of them involved with order processing and customer service. There are seven departments within the division, each headed by a department manager. Each department has its own secretary. These seven managers report to the vice-president of catalog sales, who also has a secretary. An organization chart follows:

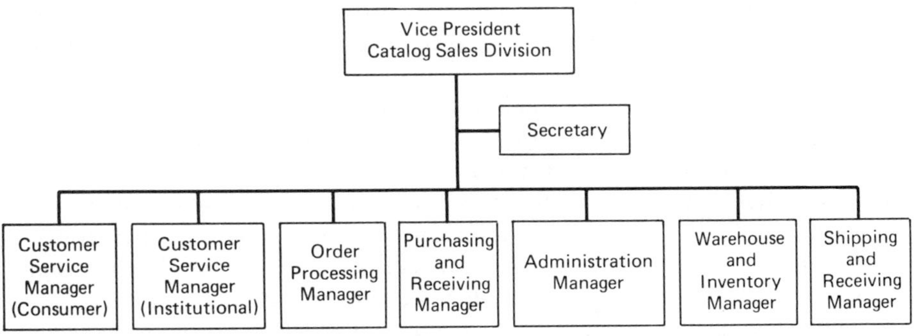

Norwich uses a batch-processing computer system to handle orders that come in by mail and phone. Orders are written up on an internal form by order entry department personnel and later (sometimes as much as five days later) the orders are keyed into the computer. People involved with inventory control have complained for a couple of years that reports about inventory levels of items in the warehouse are grossly inaccurate. The only way they can be certain what items are actually in inventory is to take a physical count. Many times the computer shows items to be in the inventory when an actual check shows Norwich has run out. The shipping department has similarly been frustrated on any number of occasions when they were given orders to fill and ship, and there was nothing to ship. Purchasing people have, on the other hand, ordered more of a certain item because they believed inventory levels to be low when, in fact, there were several months' supply on hand.

Customer service personnel experience great difficulty finding where a particular order is in the system. They repeatedly ask for the capability to give a customer a proper answer while they're on the telephone rather than having to spend time tracking down an order and then calling the customer back. Errors have been rampant in customer service's ability to tell a customer accurately when an order will be shipped. In addition, customer returns have created problems in the overall workload because of the difficulty in finding the original order.

After a number of meetings at all levels and demonstrations of equipment by several vendors, the Norwich people select an on-line computer system from Business Computers Inc. (BCI) that provides instant access to information about inventory and order status. They visited another catalog sales company in the next state that has a BCI system, and the people there are satisfied with it. However, the folks at the other company felt that the training they received from BCI was insufficient and consequently it took longer to get everyone comfortable with the system than they expected.

Two important features of the BCI system that appeal to Norwich are the word-processing and electronic-filing capabilities that will help the secretaries and its ability to provide the vice-president with a series of daily, weekly, and monthly reports on orders, shipments, inventory turnover, expenses, and profits.

It will be four months before the new equipment will be installed. Except for some of the people in the warehouse, including those in shipping and receiving, everyone will have a VDT, including management. Some managers and every secretary will have a printer. The manager of administration and her small department will have the functional responsibility for the computer and will be in charge of coordinating the overall training effort: establishing various levels of training, selecting courses or instructors, dovetailing nonvendor training with BCI, and evaluating the training itself by talking with the trainees.

Periodically throughout the next two months, the vice-president or one of the seven department managers attends a three-day seminar called "Computers and Productivity" given by the University of Chicago. The seminar is primarily for supervisors and covers

- Working theory of computers
- Batch processing versus on-line systems
- Management reports and applications
- How to attain maximum productivity
- Problems with automation
- Basic principles of word processing
- How to reduce employee fear

BCI conducts four-day training sessions at its facilities for all users. Some managers (customer service, order processing) choose to attend these classes because their departments will be heavy users of the system. All employees are encouraged to enroll in an eight-week course in basic computer science paid for by the company. Norwich also purchases five $100 hand-held computers for people to use to become acquainted with simple processing.

When the equipment is installed, BCI conducts additional training. CAI is used but instructors are present for three days to answer individual questions. About two weeks after the installation training, all departments meet individually to assess their progress and to decide on postinstallation training. BCI will conduct this training at an additional cost of $2000 per day or Norwich can use one of several consultants in the area.

You can see in our hypothetical example that the training is integrated and people-centered. Norwich as a company is making a major commitment to a new way of doing things. Management fully realizes the importance and the cost-effectiveness of training that they see as just as much a part of the automation process as the equipment and the software. Training must be a part of any overall scheme to acquire computer equipment.

In the next chapter, we'll talk about planning for technology.

Planning for Technology

Executives, managers, and supervisors hear so much about the need for planning in their organizations that many of them must feel the subject is just about worn out, but let's look at it one more time. First, we'll briefly review the reasons for and benefits of planning. Then we'll discuss how to implement your plans through proper methods of goal selection; and finally, we'll address technological planning specifically.

The Importance of Planning

It still surprises me how few the organizations that do any planning at all. People who run organizations without planning have many excuses to defend their position—"It's too difficult"; "I'm too busy"; "No one can foresee the future"; "It's a waste of time." I've found that organizations that don't plan are those constantly whipsawed by outside forces, be they competition, the government, or the economy. They are also businesses that fail to take advantage of one opportunity after another. I find that morale is usually low, productivity is less than what it could be, and there's confusion about meaningful goals. Planning *is* important, and it's important for several reasons:

1. It gives you a place to go. It's been said that if you have no destination, any road will lead you there. The *I Ching* states that it furthers one to have someplace to go. Aimlessness is not only unproductive, it isn't much fun. When Alice was lost in the woods, she suddenly came across the Cheshire cat sitting in a tree near the intersection of several roads. "Where do you want to go?" inquired the cat. "I don't know," Alice responded. The cat ended it all with, "Then it doesn't make any difference."

All people want meaning and purpose in their lives and work; you do, so do I. Part of the planning process is the setting of meaningful goals—establishing objectives. When people have something to work toward, especially when they perceive those things as good (like higher productivity), that's meaningful. They want to feel a part of their work; that's where involvement comes in.

If you have a place to go, a destination, you know when you get there. When you arrive at your destination, you can assess what you learned about getting where you want and can then set a new destination. If you have no destination, you'll never know *when* you get there.

2. We all anticipate future events, but no one can foretell the future. All we can do is envision some particular event and estimate the probability that the event will occur. But when a number of people are thinking ahead, many possibilities can be foreseen.

Suppose your department is going to get VDTs for everyone. A pregnant employee expresses strong concerns about possible radioactive emissions from the CRT and its effects on her fetus. That immediately tells you the overall plan must include information about possible health hazards, especially those affecting pregnant women.

3. It allows you and others to be creative. There's never only one way to get somewhere.

When people are allowed to explore options, they bring their creativity to bear. When you work through possibilities in advance *now*, you prevent unnecessary overreaction and surprises in the future.

4. It reduces risk and increases the probability of successfully achieving your goals.

5. Planning is a learning experience. The more you do it, the better you are at it.

6. A plan becomes a guide, a roadmap, giving you a way to get to your destination.

Planning: A Schematic Approach

Because planning is sometimes a difficult concept to visualize, let's use a simple diagram:

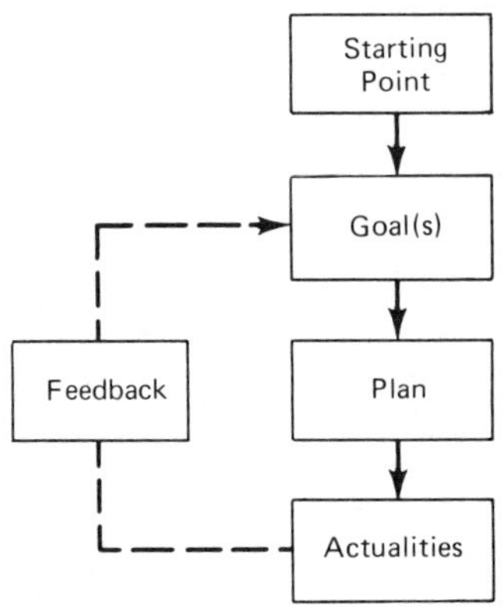

The starting point is where you are right now; it's not where you *think* you are or where you *want* to be. It consists of all the resources at your disposal—people, assets, money—and a definition of the work unit (department, division, entire organization) in as broad and generic a sense as possible. The starting point is defined more on a conceptual basis than as a limiting description of what goes on. For example, the owner of a company making garbage cans also sees his organization as a manufacturer of containers, and consequently envisions new markets for his product. He may describe what he *does* as the manufacturing of garbage cans, but how he markets his garbage cans results from expanded conceptual view of his organization as a container producer. Beginning as a container rather than garbage-can producer gives him a much broader base from which to begin planning for future development. Although you may have been part of your organization for years and think you know exactly what your organization is and does, get as much input from your employees and all available resources as possible. Like our garbage-can maker turned container baron, you may be pleasantly surprised by the untapped potential within your organization.

Goals are what people feel are important to them and their organization. To be certain, many things people want from an organization—happiness, companionship—can't be described in business terms, but if progress is being made toward reaching goals, positive feelings usually result.

Goals should be measurable by some point in time, such as a 25 percent increase in the number of forms processed in six months or a 2 percent decrease in rejected parts within seven weeks. The reason for this is so that actual performance can be analyzed. If you set a goal, you either attain it or you don't. If you don't, you either fall short of it or surpass it. In each of the three possible outcomes, it's important to know what happened along the way.

Once you establish goals, the plan itself is relatively easy to construct. It's more difficult to pinpoint meaningful goals than find the way to get there, although planning may take more time. Once a plan is underway, actualities occur that are either according to the plan or not. As goals are or are not actualized, feedback is used to change future goals if necessary.

Attaining desirable goals is also dependent on the concept of the self-fulfilling prophecy (SFP). The basic premise of the SFP is that you get what you concentrate on. If an organization is bogged down in fear, distrust, and a sense of unfulfillment, those negative feelings become part of the attempt to reach a particular goal. Consequently, the probability of reaching a goal, especially a technological one, is drastically reduced. The probability is reduced because fears constantly manifest ("Will I lose my job?") and act as braking forces to progress. If you seek goals with an attitude of positive expectation ("Not only can we do this but it's worthwhile"), the probability of success is greatly increased. The SFP is not just the power of positive thinking, which sometimes implies that the way to endure something distasteful is to force yourself to be happy about it. That kind of thinking has led to the Monday morning sales staff pep rallies with their accompanying false enthusiasm. The basis of the SFP is that *you* create the goals (prophecy) and, because you feel good about them, you throw your full support behind them.

So planning involves attitudes (emotions) as well as concrete goals. If people are a part of planning, they inevitably imbue the process with feelings of success. On the other hand, if tasks, procedures, and policies are thrust on workers by management, especially something they see as complex and technical, then attitudes will range from noncommital and apathetic to an outright desire to see the process fail. Again, involvement (love) and communication (wisdom) are the keys.

Now let's put what we've learned about planning into a multiple-step approach for introducing a new technology, specifically the acquisition of information-processing equipment.

Planning for Technology

They say a good writer, like a good salesperson, never apologizes in advance—so I won't apologize, but I will explain what I'm about to do. I'm going to go through a simple fifteen-step procedure (plan) for automation. Some of the steps may not apply to your specific organization, but this is meant to be a fairly universal approach. I'll use the word *computer* throughout even though the procedure applies to planning for all types of information processors.

Step 1: Become aware that things could be different.
Whether you have a computer system and are thinking of new hardware and software or are considering a computer for the first time, something leads you to that awareness. That something could have

been a sales call by a computer vendor, something you read, or conversations with others. In any event, what you're considering is change, one of the inevitabilities of life. Awareness is the first stage in the process of change; when we say that things could be different, we really mean things could be better.

The awareness stage should not immediately lead to the acquisition of a computer. Too many businesses, nonprofit organizations, or departments rush to get a computer without following any plan. By following a few logical steps, you can prevent one or more of the following common errors and missteps:

1. A computer may be acquired without a clear picture of how it will be used. I know of a chemical company that bought a large computer and had the equipment sitting in a hall for almost nine months while all the other preparations were being made.
2. A manager or business owner may falsely believe that once a computer is installed, all past problems will disappear. However, a computer isn't some kind of instant administrative savior; it can't improve a procedure that is already inefficient. All it can do is speed up the inefficiency.
3. An organization may acquire a system that's inadequate for its size and procedures, or the organization may grow and the computer cannot. I know of a muffler- and shock-installation business that bought a computer but had to scrap it when the business owners decided to add auto parts; the computer just couldn't handle the new inventory.
4. Computer systems that are too expensive for the organization may be leased or purchased and become a financial drain.
5. Management may fail to involve the entire department in the planning and acquisition process.
6. The workers may hold the computer in awe or, worse yet, may be afraid of it—little or no training has taken place.

The very first step, then, in acquiring a computer is to gain an awareness (not necessarily a firm, unshakable belief, but only an awareness) that things could be better. Change simply can't occur if people believe everything is perfect just the way it is. You can also think of this desire for change as constructive discontent.

You may discover that the path to technological change can be blocked. I'm not talking about an organization that looks at computers and decides the time is not right, but rather about blocks created by people who get bogged down in myths. There are lots of myths about computers:

1. Everything works fine now.
2. They're too expensive.
3. They're too complicated.
4. They'll disturb the status quo.
5. We'll lose control.

To combat these myths, a part of your awareness of change should be the awareness that certain procedures could be made more efficient (faster, more accurate) and the present staff better utilized. At this point, establish a small planning group to begin studying the situation, increase awareness, and combat the myths as they arise.

Step 2: Study current procedures.
Some people call this step a feasibility study, but I see it more as a reacquaintance with what your're doing now. It's amazing to watch organizations jump into computerization without even knowing how their present procedures are carried out. You must know where you are before you can construct an intelligent plan to get to somewhere else. Don't automatically assume you know precisely where you are; you may be mistaken.

While doing a great deal of traveling a number of years ago, I boarded a night plane for Minneapolis. When I got to my destination, I got my luggage and grabbed a yellow-and-green van with "Holiday Airport Inn" painted on its doors. When I got to the registration desk, they had no reservation for me but were able to provide a room. Because this happens relatively frequently, I thought nothing of it and went right to bed. When I checked out in the morning, I went to a waiting taxi and asked the driver to take me to Control Data Corporation. The driver looked at me strangely and then began a radio conversation with his dispatcher. After a few minutes, he turned around in his seat and asked me exactly where I wanted to go. I was a tad salty by now and responded I wanted to go to the headquarters of one of the largest employers in Minneapolis. He looked at me for about fifteen seconds and then said, "Buddy, this ain't Minneapolis, this is Denver!"

I wasn't where I thought I was—my starting point was off. You can't get to where you want if you start from someplace you aren't.

Some organizations perform the reassessment themselves, while others call in outside help, often a consultant. Some groups use a potential vendor to do a "free" study, but this invariably biases the results in favor of the vendor. I'm not against the vendor approach, but be sure you recognize its limitations; having a vendor do a review of current procedures may be putting the cart before the horse. It's generally better to know what you want a computer to do *before* you talk with software and hardware vendors. If you don't know what you want before you investigate computer systems, you may wind up shoehorning your operation into someone's computer rather than selecting the system that best suits your needs.

One warning about feasibility studies: The results invariably depend on *who* conducts the study. For example, you might think that if you were looking over your current procedures vis-à-vis possible automation, one highly probable outcome is that the department or organization needn't computerize, but that rarely seems to happen. One reason for this could be what's in the back of the minds of the people who do the studying. If only employees are used, they may realize computerization is inevitable and seek future job justification. Those who possess even latent fears that automation may cost them their jobs at a later date may literally build themselves into the new system. Vendors, as previously mentioned, have a vested interest in the outcome. Similarly, some consultants see a feasibility study as a way to generate more consulting work when the system is brought in later. You can circumvent this problem by having managers, workers, consultants, and/or vendors work together on feasibility studies. If that isn't possible, at least be aware of the possible bias that may occur if a single individual or group conducts the study.

Step 3: Determine how data flows in the organization.
In a pure sense, any organization can be thought of as a data generator. In fact, one concept computer and management information folks talk about is the data base management system (DBMS) approach. DBMS implies that any organization is nothing more than a collection of constantly changing data that, if properly managed, can provide information for decision making. If management and others know where the data comes from and where it winds up, they are in a better position to know how to put it to use more efficiently.

There are many ways to analyze data. One relatively simple method is to take the organization and divide it into functional units—most often those shown on an organization chart. Within each unit, data sources are listed along with what that data is used for.

Let's take a small manufacturing company and look at the functional unit called production:

Source of Data	Used For
Employee labor (hours and expense)	Product cost
	Productivity analysis
	Overtime reports
	Absenteeism
	Wage comparisons
	Government reports
	Payroll
Raw materials	Product cost
	Purchasing
	Inventory control
	Reject levels
Manufacturing	Product cost
	Efficiency reports
	Scrap reports
	Re-work analysis

The list could certainly be made much longer, but this gives you the general idea. You don't have to use the tabular form; some people prefer block diagrams. The method isn't as important as discovering where data generation points are and what data they produce.

Step 4: Determine what information you want.

Time and time again I see organizations that are drowning in data but starving for information. This has been a problem with computers ever since they were introduced into businesses. Because the computer works so rapidly, organizations request more and more reports, often without giving much thought to the real need for them. The trick seems to be to sift through all the available data and then to make sense of it—to transform data into information.

Because there's some confusion about the differences between data and information, let's look at a brief example. Martel Fabrics is a textile company that supplies cloth in bulk form. The company has over five hundred customers, and a typical customer record (data) looks like this:

Name:	Sportswear Fashions, Inc.	
	4600 Canoga Drive	
	Syracuse, New York 13513	
Phone:	(315) 435-2700	
Customer Number:	465101270	
Salesperson:	24	
Sales to Date:	Product 34A	$ 47,315
	Product 42B	$ 18,962
	Product 51C	$ 63,210
	Total	$129,487
Sales to Date Last Year:	Product 34A	$ 94,270
	Product 38C	$ 23,163
	Product 42B	$124,216
	Total	$241,649
Industry:	13	

I'm sure as you scan the data about Sportswear Fashions, Inc., you see many ways reports can be generated. For example, a computer containing such data on every customer can provide information relative to

1. Sales by geography (using ZIP codes or even area codes).
2. Sales by salesperson.
3. Sales by industry.
4. Sales by product—nationally, or by any of the three categories above (sales by product, by salesperson, for example).
5. Any of the above, comparing this year to date versus last year to date.
6. Changes (additions of new products and deletions of former product) by customer. For example, Sportswear Fashions, Inc., no longer purchases product 38C and now buys 51C.

7. Significant overall increases or decreases by a customer—Sportswear Fashions' purchases are considerably lower than they were a year ago.

There are more reports that can be compiled, but these seven are probably the first the sales manager for Martel will want. One effect of computerization is the temptation to keep wanting more and more information. Our sales manager may decide he wants more history relative to customer and product sales, or he may ask the accountants to provide information relative to the profitability of each product. The list goes on. Before generating more information, you should always be able to answer one question: "How am I going to *use* this information?"

Step 5: Realign or initiate new manual procedures if necessary. As a result of the study of the data sources and informational analysis, you may find that some procedures need to be changed before the computer arrives or even before you start talking with vendors. Let's suppose Martel Fabrics has a policy of sending delinquent customers to a collection agency after 180 days unless the sales manager wants special credit arrangements. During the feasibility study, the sales manager realizes that a monthly report of all customers who are more than ninety days delinquent would be helpful, but accounting is not set up to furnish this information. Consequently, accounting must formulate a procedure to provide this information *before* computerization occurs. If the system is not set up to provide the information manually (for example, if accounting does not collect the right data to generate the information), the computer won't be able to do so either.

Step 6: Investigate software first, hardware second.
I have watched the reverse of this for years: Someone buys a computer and then looks around for something for it to do. Can you imagine hiring people like that? The reason you go through Step 4 (determining the data flow) and Step 5 (discovering the information you want or the processes you want to automate) is to enable you to look for the software that does the job you want. Sometimes you can find packaged (canned) software that fits your needs. The spread-sheet or financial projection programs like Visicalc and Supercalc are widely known examples of this approach.

Canned software tends to be used by smaller organizations, such as small businesses and professional practices. For example, I talk to veterinarians across the country describing the advantages, disadvantages, and proper use of a computer in animal hospitals or clinics. There are forty-three vendors of software systems for veterinarians, and most of the vendors also offer hardware. I found somewhat the same situations with bookstores—there are about ten vendors having software or software-and-hardware systems specifically designed for booksellers.

Sometimes you can find packaged software that can be changed to fit your operation. Normally these changes are made by the software vendor for an additional fee, but sometimes the user can make the changes.

The final type of software is that which must be created from scratch. Again, this can be done by an outside vendor, a programmer hired by the organization for this purpose, trained company personnel, or a combination of these.

To be sure, many times you will be looking at software and hardware at the same time, but concentrate on the software first. Once you find adequate canned software or a way to create your own, look at the machinery. Hardware today is pretty much the same, although improvements hit the street daily and manufacturers come and go. It's important that hardware comes from a reliable manufacturer, one who can be counted on to be in business five years from now. Because some vendors put their own labels on computers, make sure to find out who actually manufactures the machine.

The service component—training, maintenance, furnishing program updates—is far more important than the hardware—as IBM found out to its betterment and Osborne discovered to its detriment. One of the most important pieces of information vendors provide is a list of installations where their systems are operating now. Visit these places and talk to both users and managers. They are valuable sources of information regarding both hard- and software selection.

Step 7: Gain knowledge of computer systems.
If your department or organization is going to be committed to computerization in one form or another, everyone in it needs to know computers—not as intimately as programmers or computer engineers know them, but at the working knowledge level. People should know what a byte is, how a disk works, that the inner workings of a computer consist mostly of tiny switches.

We've already discussed a number of ways this knowledge can be gained (vendor training, local school, CAI, consultant). Remember: Management must be committed to the process of education and training.

Step 8: Justify the computer.
Justification occurs in two ways—operationally and financially. The first is a piece of cake if you've done your homework properly. If you know what you want from a computer, the system that comes the closest to this is the one that's operationally justified. A case of a nonjustified system occurs when hardware is purchased with little idea what it's supposed to do.

Financial justification may take a little more doing, but often the vendor can help you. It isn't complicated, but it does take a little thinking on your part. It's important because the major reason for automation is an increase in revenue, a decrease in costs, or both. When we speak of efficiency and effectiveness, we are really speaking of money.

Probably the simplest kind of financial justification relates to people. Although most automation systems don't immediately put people out of work, they often do remove the need to hire additional personnel to meet a growing workload. (Even if there is eventually an opportunity to reduce staff, this is best done through normal attrition). For example, if a computer system precludes the hiring of two people with average annual salary and benefits of $15,000 each, that's a savings of $30,000 a year. If you select a 2½ year* favorable payback period, as long as the total cost of the system is less than $75,000 (2.5 times $30,000) it's financially justified.

If you prefer a more thorough analysis, you must analyze each function the computer will improve and estimate the financial value of that improvement. Let's look at a typical small business with the following characteristics:

Sales:	$1,000,000
Accounts Receivable:	$100,000†
Accounts Payable:	$150,000†
Inventory:	$200,000†
Profit (before tax):	10percent

Based on evidence from other automated businesses, we find that computer-assisted management of both accounts receivable and accounts payable increases revenues (not sales) by 5 percent of their average annual values (although I have heard of percentages as high as 10 to 15 percent). Regarding inventory control, a very conservative estimate is a 10 percent cost savings from more timely purchases as a result of computerization. We can also assume this new computer system will increase sales by 6 percent with the use of word-processing software for promotion and customer information. Therefore, the overall financial effect of computerization is:

Receivables:	5% × $100,000	$ 5,000
Payables:	5% × $150,000	7,500
Inventory:	10% × $200,000	20,000
Profit increase:	6% × 10% × $1,000,000	6,000
	TOTAL	$38,500

If we apply the 2½ year payback period to the $38,500, we have a maximum system cost of $96,250.

Office procedures are handled the same way. Most of these savings come from increased work output, but something like electronic filing greatly reduces the lost time looking for something that's been misfiled

---

*This is relatively arbitrary but reflects the average time most accountants feel comfortable with.

†These are annual averages.

in a drawer. Teleconferencing eliminates travel cost for meetings plus reduces time away from the job. If there are four people working in an office and a computer system can increase the productivity by 25 percent, that's like having one more person working without pay.

I didn't do a discounted cash flow analysis bringing in depreciation, tax credits, and the like, although it's not difficult and usually makes the financial results look better. However, I like to keep the analysis as simple as possible, at least in the beginning. These financial determinations of increased revenue and decreased cost are done before the equipment is brought in and can actually be performed before a final system is chosen. Used in this way, such financial analysis can help set limits on the cost of the computer. When the final system is chosen and all costs known, the accountants can perform their wizardry regarding discounted cash flows and internal rates of return.

Step 9: Sign the contract for the system you want.
Read the contract before you sign it. This sounds like such simple advice, yet many problems arise because the purchasers didn't do this. Consequently, many of their problems later on with the vendor are the result of their misunderstanding the terms of the contract rather than the vendor reneging on the agreement. I don't think you need a lawyer in on the deal, but you should go over each clause carefully and ask questions about those that are not clear. Although the following list is by no means exhaustive, here are a few things to look for:

1. What are the responsibilities of the vendor regarding installation of the equipment, training, and maintenance?
2. What are the responsibilities of the customer?
3. How many hours of training are "free" with the system? How many people can be trained under the contract? Where will this training take place? What is the cost of additional training by the vendor?
4. Can the customer make adaptations to the system?
5. Is the software guaranteed? What will the vendor do if it doesn't do what it's supposed to do? Will the vendor supply software updates free of charge for some period of time?
6. What happens if the vendor creates new software? Is this free?
7. What if the vendor goes out of business? What precautions have been taken? (Most vendors are willing to put a copy of the source code—actual program—in the hands of a third party, such as an attorney.)
8. If a maintenance clause or separate contract is involved, what is the monthly cost now and in the future? If maintenance is not provided by the vendor, who does it?
9. What recourse is available to the customer if the system does not function as claimed?

Also important to both customer and vendor is the manner of acquisition—rental, lease, or purchase. Rentals, which aren't too prevalent, are short-term arrangements. Equipment can normally be returned to the vendor with thirty days' notice; because of this, the monthly rental is substantially higher than when the equipment is leased.

Leases are long-term arrangements and typically run from three to five years. The normal rule for estimating the monthly lease price is to take the entire cost of the computer system as quoted by the vendor and divide by forty for a five-year lease. Remember, this is only a guide and actual cases may vary. Larger vendors (IBM, A. B. Dick) often provide leasing themselves; smaller vendors often work directly with third-party leasing companies. Typically, a five-year lease runs for sixty months and then a single payment at the end of the period (such as one more month's payment or a percent of the original purchase price) allows the customer to own the equipment outright. Again, the contract should spell out these conditions in detail. It's a good idea to check with your accountant or finance department regarding the IRS's current stand regarding such ever-changing things like tax credits which may influence your decision whether or not to lease.

The final method of acquisition is outright purchase. Large organizations often pay cash for their system, whereas smaller ones may secure a commercial bank loan, with many banks willing to loan up to 80 percent of the total value of the system.

Probably the most unique method of acquisition I've come across was used by a manufacturing client of mine. When I asked my client how he was going to pay for the $32,000 system, he said he would do it with raw materials. It took me a minute to realize that because he was in the jewelry business, one of his raw materials was gold. Off he marched to his local bank like a century-old Klondiker with his poke of gold.

Step 10: Plan the installation with the vendor.
There will (hopefully) be some time between the signing of the contract and the delivery of the equipment. During this time, planning is not only necessary with the vendor, but with all involved personnel. The vendor should be able to provide a schedule regarding the time necessary to train your people, to install the equipment, and to have the system fully operational. At this time you must also consider

1. Where the equipment will be located
2. Who will have what pieces of equipment
3. What supplies (paper, forms, floppy disks) will be needed
4. What types of supporting equipment (special furniture, anti-static pads, power controllers) will be required
5. Who will be in charge of the system
6. Special environmental needs—electrical power, heat and humidity, decor
7. Possible physical changes in the office layout

Another consideration to address at this time is the entire process of conversion from a manual system to an automated one. There is usually a period of parallel operation when both manual and automated systems run simultaneously. This allows users to ease into new procedures while still maintaining, but gradually loosening the ties to the former system. This cut-over may take several weeks, months, or even a year depending on the complexity of the change.

The important point is to lay all this out in advance so that disruption and confusion are reduced to a minimum and employee satisfaction and positive expectations are increased.

Step 11: Install the computer.

The time to install the computer system is when everyone is ready. It's that simple. If the pre-installation training and education are properly carried out and the overall plan is more or less unfolding the way people want and expect, the installation is rapid and without problems. The vendor normally installs the equipment in two phases. The first phase is physical installation: running wires and cables, placing VDTs, and housing pieces of equipment such as hard disks and central processors. This can take hours or weeks. The second phase, a full check of the system to be certain it is functioning correctly, begins once the hardware is in place. This two-phase installation ensures that the hardware works the way it's supposed to and that the software system performs the proper tasks.

Training takes place during the installation. Not everyone needs to know where all the cables are, but someone within the organization should work with the vendor on the physical system. As the software is "brought up" (made operable), users of the equipment should be in on the process. I see far too many computer systems fail to reach their full potential because operators are not knowledgeable about how the system came to be. Operator education is also a vital part of reducing employee fear and increasing confidence. If you ever have been to an automobile factory and watched a car being assembled from scratch, the entire concept of a completed car is not nearly so mysterious to you. You still may not be able to fix one or even understand the theory of its operation, but you feel more knowledgeable and more confident.

During the installation, it might be feasible and advantageous to have vendor personnel work hand-in-hand with your own people as the software is checked out. Talk about this with the vendor.

Step 12: Enter data.

For some organizations, especially those making the transition from manual or semiautomated (bookkeeping machines, batch-processing computers) to full, on-line, multitasking automated systems, entering data may be an arduous task. For a fully automated system to reach its full potential, all historic and current data must be placed onto the computer's hard or floppy disks. This can be accomplished in one of several ways. Some organizations want to do this all at once. One professional practice I know brought in a team of outside data-entry people and had the information on 12,000 patients keyed in over a weekend. On Friday night, the computer was empty, and by Monday morning the system had all the necessary data and was ready to go. There was one problem, however. Because the data entry people were not familiar with medical terminology, taking into account that for some unknown reason medical people don't always have the most legible handwriting, they created hundreds of new diseases. The computer could not tell that ovariohysterectomy was the same as ovariahysterectomy, the latter being merely an error in reading someone's handwriting.

If you do choose to use outsiders, sometimes the larger vendors can provide people to do this, or they may be able to recommend a service bureau to do the job if they can't. Some of the temporary-help companies like Kelly or Olsten also have people available that specialize in data entry. Another possibility is to hire high school or college students on a part-time basis.

My own recommendation is to have everyone (*everyone*, not just the administrative people) spend time entering data. I certainly don't suggest that the CEO of a multimillion-dollar company spend hours in front of a VDT punching in words and numbers, but he or she should have some exposure to it.

If the job is done in-house and gradually, it can often dovetail directly with the parallel operation of manual and automated systems, thereby easing that transition. Depending on many factors, the data-entry job can take anywhere from a few days to a year.

Step 13: Get the first program running.
Many of the systems sold today consist of a number of programs. Sometimes these programs are integrated, as is the case with a total accounting package consisting of accounts payable, accounts receivable, inventory, payroll, and the general ledger. If a small business purchases such a system, they often focus on getting one part of the package running—the payroll program, for example. In a full word-processing system including electronic filing, perhaps the automated typing feature is the first program to be mastered.

Pay attention to the vendor's recommendations and check with others who have already traveled the path you're embarking on. I prefer to see the task approached in a step-wise fashion, but I do recognize that there are swimmers who prefer to approach chilly water by jumping in rather than taking it an inch at a time. If you're one of these, go ahead and do everything at once. However, be sure your workers agree with your approach. Otherwise, they'll be frustrated and dissatisfied with both you and the equipment. Remember: They're the ones who will utimately be spending the most time with the system, even though your involvement may appear to be more extensive at the beginning. Even though you think your more aggressive approach saves time now, it may cost you dearly in the future.

92

Step 14: Get the entire system operational.

In theory, this phase may never be attained because there are new breakthroughs in hardware and software occurring every day. However, what I'm referring to is having every program, every piece of software that's part of the original acquisition, running the way everyone expects or, if it doesn't, knowing the reason why. I add that last phrase because sometimes particular problems arise while the system is becoming operational that weren't foreseen. Sometimes these are items that are simply overlooked. A manufacturing company ran into difficulty because its customer number was thirteen alphanumeric characters long and the vendor's program only allowed eight numerical digits and no letters. If the overall plan your people and the vendor put together is carefully thought out, the "what-ifs" will be considered in advance. It's not as important to hit a particular date for full operation right on the nose as it is to know why a delay occurred and how similar ones may be prevented in the future.

If you have 80 percent of the system up and running by the time you thought you'd be fully operational, you've done very well, especially if it's your first time through.

Step 15: Continue to assess your computer needs.

Let's begin with two approaches you should *not* take after your system is running properly, and both are extremes. Don't assume that what you have is exactly what you will/must stay with forever. Anywhere from three to seven years after you acquire a computer system, you'll replace it. That's simply the way things seem to be. If you buy a truck and plan to use it all day every day, you don't expect that vehicle still to be around in ten years. A computer is an asset with a limited life. And don't expect to have an asset with much resale value in seven years either. At a college where I taught, the best deal we could get for our old computer was from a scrap dealer who wanted $400 to pick it up and cart it away!

The other wrong approach occurs when an organization goes computer crazy and tries to add every new whistle and bell it can to an existing system in a frantic effort to get the most out of it. This process usually creates havoc because no one ever seems able to keep up with all the new additions.

The best approach is to have a small group of users and managers continually assess organizational requirements. This doesn't mean only hardware and software requirements, but also training needs as well. The vendor can be a valuable source of information for possible improvements and additions to the current system as long as the assessing group can distinguish between those things the vendor wants to sell and those that will actually benefit the organization and the system.

As I've said before, things always change, but by continually reevaluating your system, such changes need never be surprises.

Summary

Let's summarize the fifteen steps to use when planning for a new technology:

1. Gain an awareness that things could be different—that is, better.
2. Study current procedures.
3. Determine how data flows in the organization.
4. Determine what information you want.
5. Realign or initiate new manual procedures if necessary.
6. Investigate all aspects of the equipment. For example, when considering computers, investigate the software first, then the hardware.
7. Gain knowledge of equipment systems.
8. Justify the equipment.
9. Sign the contract for the system you want.
10. Plan the installation with the vendor.
11. Install the equipment.
12. Enter data.
13. Get the first program running.
14. Get the entire system operational.
15. Continue to assess your equipment needs.

Type this list and and use it as a reminder if necessary when you begin to automate. Although all of the fifteen steps may not pertain to your particular operation or proposal acquisition, the majority will or can be adapted to suit your needs.

At the end of Chapter 3, we saw how John Sykes and his people at Stratford Distributors approached the acquisition of a new computer. Look again at Figure 3-1 on page 47; notice that the Stratford group uses twelve steps rather than fifteen. I strongly suggest you use a chart such as Figure 3-1 to do your overall planning. Make it big enough to hang on a wall and let everyone refer to it. Use actual dates along the bottom; cut out of construction paper a big red arrow and move the arrow along the bottom of the chart as the days pass. This isn't meant to be cute or childish; it's an effective way to help you and your people visualize progress toward a goal.

In the beginning of this chapter, we discussed the value of seeing planning as a roadmap to get to your destination or goal. The more a goal can be visualized, the more likely its attainment. This has been proven time and again in all kinds of places from the psychology laboratory to the factory. We've all seen those thermometers that keep getting painted in red at higher and higher levels as a community or nonprofit group raises money for a specific goal. The rising "temperature" works. The little red arrow or anything else you and your people dream up to help you mark your progress will undoubtedly work as long as the attitude is proper. If the attitude (or morale, if you prefer) is positive and everyone views the computer as an enhancement, the goals will be reached and everyone will feel even better about themselves and their jobs. If, on the other hand, management unilaterally decides to get a computer and foist it on the workers with a bunch of directives and no real plan, chaos and ill will is assured.

People will feel like robots.

They will be.

Now, let's hammer it home again. People want to be cared for. They want to know they're needed. I saw soldiers in Vietnam face near-certain death because of a love for those around them and belief in their goals. You show people they're needed by involving them in what's going on, asking for their opinion, and soliciting their advice. You don't have to do everything they suggest; they understand that. But be sure to get them in on any plan to get a computer system. Remember: To some people, computers are downright frightening.

The other thing people want is communication. They want to know what's happening. They're not prying or looking for secrets (but they might if information is constantly withheld). Talk to them.

Well, it's love (a need to be needed) and wisdom (communication) all over again. As Charlie Brown would say, "Sigh."

Systems Already in Existence

8

I'm certain there are those of you who are saying, "This stuff's okay, but what about me? I already have a system and I don't think it's working out very well. What can I do?" That's a very good question, and it deserves an equally good answer. First of all, bear in mind that it's *never* too late to start doing things differently. Second, remember that attitude plays a large part in the success of any change; people, especially managers, must be committed to the change. Finally, be sure it's the system and not you that needs to change. For instance, it's never too late to initiate training, but if your people don't trust you and your decisions, instituting a training program may be seen as unnecessary or negative—management forcing employees to go to "school" to get more work out of them. Managers must have infectious enthusiasm about change and must demonstrate high expectations regarding new results. Nothing is ever so bad that it can't be changed.

If you already have a computer system, it was probably put in while you were with the organization or you inherited it. If you were a part of a group that brought in a computer system you now consider inadequate, you may have to deal with peers and superiors before any changes can be made. How you handle this depends on you and your organization. If yours is the kind of organization that welcomes suggestions for change, you don't have to worry much about embarrassing people. Whether you're talking to superiors, peers, or your workers, no one should feel they didn't do their job properly in the past. Not recognizing certain things in the beginning is no one's fault; blaming people is counterproductive to change as well as being a waste of time.

If you inherit a system—you're hired to fill a particular position and the computer's already in place—it's often easier to make changes because new people are expected to bring new insights. You still may be faced with the problem of making others, or rather their decisions, look bad, but simply approach the issue with the attitude that people did their best at the time and things can always be improved.

Where to Start

There are many places to start, but I prefer to evaluate the system first in terms of what changes, if any, are seen as necessary or beneficial by those who use it. You may want to talk with the users individually, in a group, or solicit their written comments. Whatever approach you choose, remember that people may initially be reluctant to be openly critical but after a few of the braver souls begin, the well-known streaming effect takes place.

You can gather your information via a structured questionnaire or simply ask users what they like and don't like about the system. If you use the structured approach, here are a few sample questions:

1. Do you understand as much as you want about the basic operation of the computer system itself?
2. Did you receive sufficient training on the use of the system? If not, what was lacking?
3. Is the hardware easy to use? Are there improvements that can be made?
4. Has the equipment performed reliably? How many times has your particular system or terminal malfunctioned? Was the problem rectified quickly?
5. Has the vendor supported the system properly?
6. Does the equipment create any physical discomforts for you? If so, what do you think could be done to make it more comfortable?
7. Are there environmental conditions—office decor, layout of equipment— that could be improved?
8. Does the software work the way it's supposed to? Are there problems with it? Can you work with it easily?
9. Do you believe that the system improves your job? If not, what things are worse?
10. Are there any fears or misgivings you have regarding the system?
11. If there were only one change you could make, what would it be?

If your people trust you and you conduct your survey with care, you'll have a fair idea what changes, if any, are necessary. You'll also come to one of the following conclusions:

1. The people are satisfied with the system and their own personal situation.
2. The system operates satisfactorily but there's a need for additional training, relocation of equipment, ergonomic furniture.
3. The system itself is inadequate but can be upgraded or changed to improve both attitudes and performance.
4. The system is unsatisfactory and can't be changed.
5. Some people are unable to use the system or are antagonistic toward it; however, most find the system adequate.

The Next Step

If the system is operating well and people are satisfied with their work, you have a truly enviable condition; all you and your people have to do is to keep looking for improvements. If the system is satisfactory but some improvements are needed, you and your people can begin planning the changes.

If the system is marginal but can be upgraded, go back to the original vendor and explain the changes you want to make. Ask the vendor what is required to make the changes (new terminals, screens, faster CPU), and so on) and get a written estimate of the cost. What if the original vendor can't provide what you want? Let's assume your organization has word-processor VDTs that produce eyestrain, fatigue, and headaches. One of your employees reads that there are terminals whose screens display information in black print on a white background similar to a typed page. It's possible that the original vendor dosen't have such terminals; therefore, another vendor must be found, one who produces VDTs compatible with the existing system and your employees' needs.

You may find that your system is simply not the right one and nothing within reason can be done to improve the situation. Assuming you don't want to continue with an inadequate system, you must make a change. Some people go back to a manual system. There's nothing wrong with this as long as it's what people want, it's possible to do (which it may not be), and people don't sour on computers in general just because this one didn't work out. If you go back to a manual system, keep an open mind regarding future automation.

It's also important to learn why the whole thing went haywire; many times we learn more from our failures than our successes. Remember the people factor in your analysis: Were they alienated at the start? Take a look at the procedures existing prior to automation: Did the organization try to automate something that was already faulty or inefficient? Was the system itself at fault? Was the hardware or software too limited? Some businesses begin computerization with a floppy disk system when they really need the storage capacity of a hard disk. Sometimes initially adequate hardware and software keeps getting built up as the organization's needs expand until finally efficiency suffers. For example, many businesess keep adding more internal memory to their computers to store increased data. After a while, the search time is so long, the computer literally slows down. Others go programming crazy, continually hooking new programs to old ones in an effort to upgrade a software system that should be replaced. The result is an inefficient tangled maze of subroutines; the software simply can't do what it's supposed to do. Lesson for next time: Plan well.

If you decide you need a new system, normally you just can't run right out and buy one. For example, there may have to be some financial planning or budgetary approval. Furthermore, feasibility studies and planning are particularly necessary when replacing an existing system. But once you start the ball rolling, be sure to involve your people and keep them informed. If delays are possible, tell them. Let them know they may have to struggle along as best they can for a while, but also that you're aware of their problems. Make sure they realize it's going to take a while to do the job right.

What if it's strictly a people problem? What do you do when you discover there may be people who simply can't or won't work with a functioning system for their own reasons? If these individuals can't be helped sufficiently to overcome their reasons, you may have to consider removing them from your organization if they do not choose to leave of their own accord. Possibly a transfer to another department can solve the problem, but if you're a smaller organization that doesn't have "another department," you may have to consider letting some people go. In short, you may have to fire some people and hire more compatible replacements.

When People Quit or You Fire Them

People leave organizations—they die, take leaves of absence of all kinds (for example, health), retire, get laid off, quit, get fired. We're going to talk about the last two reasons because they're the ones that create the most problems. What do you do, how do you feel when automation results in people quitting or being fired?

When someone leaves your group, section, department, or division of their own accord, it gives you a magnificent opportunity to learn how your people view you and what you do. Some supervisors get angry and fearful when one of their subordinates quits; they want to strike back somehow, to downgrade that person or his or her performance in some way. But when people quit, it's invariably because they believe whatever they're going to do—another job, their own business, school, nonwork activity—is better for them. That's the only reason. If you love your people you want them to be happy and can only share their joy. If you're open and honest with your employees, you can use this opportunity for more feedback on how you're perceived as a manager—both good points as well as those requiring improvement. If a departing employee says, "You know, Claire, you don't keep people informed about what's going on," that isn't a reason to get angry. If the comment raises a question in your mind, ask others about the situation. If they agree, you may choose to do something about it. For example, by creating the belief that people feel better and are more productive when they are informed, Claire can become more aware of the need for communication.

Most exit interviews are about as useful as the policy manual that creates them. Too often they're done by a form-filler-outer in the personnel department whose sole job seems to be to vouchsafe the fullness of employee folders. Even when something major is detected—like one supervisor's magnificent or bestial treatment of subordinates—little is done about it. More data. More files.

Hold your own "exit interview," but make it a parting conversation. Do it over lunch or dinner. *You treat!* Ask meaningful questions like "What's the biggest single problem in our department? The organization?" or "What upset you the most on your job?" "Was technology difficult for you, even fearful?" Encourage and support honesty. Don't alibi for anything. If you were unable to get this person the raise he expected once the computer was in and running and he says that's the reason he's leaving, simply tell him what happened. Don't make excuses for yourself or for others.

Firing someone is another subject entirely. I don't mean "permanent lay-offs because there's no work"; I don't mean "outplacement"—I mean firing someone. Sacking him. Giving him his walking papers. Although this should be your right and your responsibility as a manager, unfortunately some organizations get union arbitrators, personnel departments, or ombudsmen involved in a process that often becomes dehumanizing and unnecessarily complicated.

Someday you'll have to fire someone. That's a given. You don't have to do it with malice; you don't have to be tense, unpleasant, or even sorry about it. If you can realize that you're helping the person, you can feel anything you want to, including joy.

Firing someone dosen't have to involve mental anguish for either you or your employee. In almost every management seminar I conduct, I reach a point where I ask how many people have ever been fired. About 25 percent of the participants, including me, raise their hands. When I ask several individuals to reflect on the situation and give their present views on it, more than one always responds that they now realize that it was *the best thing that ever happened to them!* It didn't seem so at the time, but as their path in life evolved, they recognized what a great opportunity the firing gave them to change.

When people are happy about themselves and their work, they perform well. If either work-related personal problems or their work is dissatisfying, their performance suffers. Are you doing anyone a favor by keeping them in a position in which they're unhappy? Is the lure of the paycheck and benefits so great that anyone really wants to stay in a position in which their unhappiness results in inferior work?

When you fire someone, do it with love and true concern. Your subordinate may experience stress, but there's no need for you to contribute to it. Gently but honestly tell the person the reason for the firing as you perceive it; don't cover up anything. This may be tough because generally we don't fire people for incompetence, we fire them for "personal reasons" or "politics." These terms are used by both managers and employees, but they don't really mean anything to either one. What are your real reasons for firing Helen and Joe? Isn't it really Helen's unwillingness to share the word processor with Debbie in spite of all your requests? Isn't it really because the computer system requires a full complement of personnel to run it efficiently and Joe's negative feeling about computerization in general is demoralizing to everyone? Then say so. If they choose to tell their friends you fired them for political or personal reasons, that's fine; but as a good manager you owe it to them and their future development to be as specific and honest as possible.

After you explain your reasons, give your employee an opportunity to be equally honest with you. Although those who are fired are often more emotional than those who quit, they also can be valuable sources of insight into how others view you and your organization. Listen objectively; it may keep you from mismatching person and job in the future.

Help the person you fire make the transition. Get him or her at least a month's severance pay, even two. Find out about state and federal unemployment benefits and good employment agencies in the area. Offer your help, including acting as a reference if you feel you can be objective. If you're called for a reference about a person you fired, stress his or her good points. Be honest about the firing situation. Point out that the situation (1) was in the past, and (2) was between you and him or her; it doesn't mean the same thing will happen in the future.

Removing the guilt and hostility from firing in no way decreases the significance of the act. It is a major event for both you and your employee; but done in a sensitive and caring way, it can be a positive learning experience for you both.

Hiring New People

There's no excuse for not hiring the best people available for a job or position. True, there are all kinds of government regulations that seem to restrict a manager's free choice in the hiring process, and some overly zealous administrators of such programs have done a disservice to many employers, but the choice is still yours. You can hire a less qualified person, then cop out and say "the government (or the boss) made me do it," or you can defend your view that you want the best section, department, agency, or organization that can be had. Most successful managers place a high priority on the selection of people because they know that having the best can only improve efficiency in the long run.

If you're in the process of looking for someone—for example, a data-entry clerk or dp manager—you probably first become acquainted with that person in the form of a piece of paper, or maybe several pieces. It's a shame that thinking, feeling human beings are reduced to a resumé or a few brief notes on a job application, but so far it's still the most efficient way to introduce an employer to a large number of prospective employees in a short time. We'll limit our discussion to the normal pre-employment cycle of application (or resumé)-interview-offer, and not the exceptions such as hiring someone from another department within the organization, or trying to woo someone away from another employer (which can border on the unethical and lead to future catastrophes if not properly handled).

Collecting resumés can be frustrating. For example, if you place a display ad in Tuesday's *Wall Street Journal*, you may receive 5000 resumes by Friday in the mail. Even an ad in the local paper can create problems. If you list your company's name and address, you'll be spending a lot of time on the phone, plus dealing with drop-in candidates, especially if it's a minor position. Some of the employment agencies ("body shops," "flesh peddlers") will call, extolling the virtues of one of their wares. The deluge can be overwhelming. Where do you begin?

One screening technique I like for supervisory and skilled job openings is the use of a reputable employment agency. There are now such agencies that specialize in people with computer backgrounds. Then I visit the agency and describe the available position to the people on their placement staff. This gives the counselors and me an opportunity to get to know each other. As they refer candidates, I let them know my assessment of each one. If I reject someone, I tell them why so they can become more accurate in finding the person I'm looking for.

If you find yourself in the resumé-reading business, these hints from a friend and colleague of mine, Don Baggs, president of Career Crossroads in Brattleboro, Vermont, are helpful. Don sees a resumé as having three qualities a prospective employer should look for: appearance, criteria, and content.

Appearance

1. Is it prepared neatly on quality paper with no obvious typographical errors?
2. Is the copy clean and easy to read, or is it a copy of a copy of a copy?
3. Is it overly pretentious—colored paper or ink, fancy border, oversized paper?

Criteria

1. Does it tell the story quickly?
2. Are there concrete examples of accomplishments? (Some resumés only list duties, not what the subject actually did.)
3. Is there a fair smattering of action-oriented words such as *planned, organized, instituted?*
4. What results has the subject had? Has he or she been successful in reaching goals?

Content

1. Is the resumé focused? Is it apparent what the writer wants to do?
2. Are there unexplained time gaps?
3. Has the individual exhibited growth in his or her life's work?
4. Has there been a reasonable length of tenure (more than one year) in each of the positions?
5. Has the individual evidenced self-improvement through training?
6. Is there a lot of irrelevant information?

Basically, a resumé is a sales brochure for a unique product. As such, it can be a negative or positive indicator about the person it describes. Some seasoned managers can spot resumés prepared by resumé services, and often reject those out of hand. Their philosophy is that they would rather have a less-than-perfect brochure done by the subject himself than a slick piece of work done by a professional. However, that's a matter of individual preference.

Once you select the individuals whose applications or resumés indicate they have the skills and qualities you want, the next step is the interview, the keystone of the hiring process. Some managers dread interviewing, and if they do, it usually shows. Interviewing or, better yet, conversing with a stranger is a wonderful opportunity to meet a new person, even make a new friend. Even if the session doesn't result in that person's joining your organization, both of you can gain understanding and a sense of sharing from the experience. Enter conversation with that objective and the process goes along much more smoothly. Compare this to those approaches where you begin by asking, "Why do you want to work for me?" Chances are the person has no idea why he or she wants to work for you; he or she probably doesn't even know you.

By keeping the conversation open and informal, you accomplish much more than if you adhere to a rigid structure. Remember: About 95 percent of the technical part of any job in this country can be done by nearly anyone, and few people get fired for technical incompetency.

Most people get fired because of interpersonal conflicts: how the person relates to you and others. Find out how people think and feel in addition to what they can do, and you'll have a much better idea what to expect from them.

There are entire books devoted to methods for interviewing people. Some recommend all kinds of support data from simple intelligence tests (whatever they are) to using lie detectors to full-day psychoanalysis at the $200-per-hour shrink. Most of this "data" is a crutch for those who lack confidence in their ability to interview and hire. You do the interviewing; you make the decision. This person isn't going to work with the psychiatrist; he or she is going to work with you.

The most important key to good interviewing is to be your normal, relaxed self. Let the conversation drift around a bit. If you're nervous, your subject will be, too. Encourage questions. Be supportive. If the dialogue falters, there's one simple technique you can use to fill what might otherwise be embarrassing gaps in the conversation. When your speaker pauses, encourage him or her to continue by taking his or her last phrase or sentence and turning it into a question.

For example, if your candidate is describing his or her education and ends with, " ... after high school I took some courses in economics," all you have to do is ask, "Economics?" That simple question will usually encourage more explanation. You also can use some of the following conversation starters:

"What did you learn from that experience?"

"Tell me more about that."

"What did you do then?"

"Oh?"

"Yes?"

After the interviews, it's time to make a choice. Too many managers get hung up with *things*—salary, degrees, direct experience, past titles—and forget the person. Base your choice on *who you want*. You know the answer to that question; it's the easiest choice to make. If you're right, the person will want the job as much as you want him or her. The details, the things can be worked out.

Trust your feelings. They're important.

When you hire people, especially newcomers into a highly technical environment, don't abandon them. Many supervisors think they're too busy to spend time with a new employee when indeed it's one of their most important activities. Can you remember your first day on the job? What things would you have *liked* to happen?

Ignoring this responsibility can create a lot of problems down the line. I once got myself into a peck of trouble on a new job because my boss didn't bother to spend some time with me at the beginning. After three days as the marketing research manager for a precision metal goods manufacturer, I could find my office, my secretary's, and the men's room. So I decided to venture forth and get a cup of coffee from the machine in the employees' cafeteria. I brought the coffee back to my office and continued working. Several minutes later, my boss stuck his head in my office. His face changed from a pleasant expression to one of horror. He pointed at the half-full cup.

"What is that?" he asked heatedly.

"It's a cup of coffee," I replied.

"What's it doing there?" he demanded.

I was a bit befuddled and answered with something stupid like, "Everything has to be somewhere." As he became angrier, I became more confused. I asked him what the problem was. Then the light dawned. Hadn't anyone explained that drinking coffee at the workplace, even in a private office, wasn't allowed? No.

Several years earlier, the company hired a vice-president of manufacturing. During his first week on the job, he noticed a number of his machine operators drinking coffee while they worked, a violation of company policy he had been thoroughly familiarized with. He put an immediate stop to this and issued a memo to every manufacturing department that the only time to drink coffee was during scheduled coffee breaks. He even instituted loud claxons in the plant to signal the start and finish of breaks. Well, people being the way they are, it wasn't long before manufacturing people noticed that other employees from sales, purchasing, accounting, and personnel were getting coffee whenever they wanted. A hue and cry went up that finally reached the president's office. The president then issued a peace-keeping order that *all* employees, including senior vice-presidents, must abide by the ten-minute break routines.

The point is, I don't think any of the illicit coffee drinkers initially did it to antagonize their superiors. Like me, they were ignorant of the rule because no one took the time to familiarize them properly with company policy. It was only when they were criticized that they became antagonistic. As the employees flaunted their coffee cups, management's response became equally bizarre, and a vicious cycle began. How well I remember secretly brewing coffee in my desk long after the claxon had sounded the end of the break. True, there's no excuse for ignorance, but as a good manager, it's your responsibility to provide the environment for learning.

The following list of questions gives you a few guidelines regarding that critical first day:

1. What things would I like to know if I were new that would make me feel more comfortable and "at home"?
2. What impressions do I, as a supervisor, want to make on the new person?
3. What *key* policies and procedures should I explain to the new person so that mistakes will not be made on the second day?

4. How can I help the new employee begin to know his or her fellow employees without feeling overwhelmed?
5. What physical things does this person need (desk, work area, VDT)?
6. What job-related things can I teach the new person? Is it possible for them to achieve "something" on their first day?
7. What single positive experience can I provide?
8. How can I ensure that I will be available for most of the day?
9. How can I ensure that others (my boss, personnel department) will also be available on the first or, at least, the second day?

Summary

We've talked about some possible solutions to situations where a computer system isn't appropriate for an organization, its needs, and its people. Although we discussed firing people as one solution for mismatched computer-employee pairs, firing is never the easy way out, nor should it be. It's a last resort. Perhaps people just aren't working to capacity and enjoying it because of faulty management practices that can be cured with a little love and attention. Because the practice of management is so important, we'll spend the next chapter talking about management today and the effects of computerization on it now and in the future.

Humane Management in a Technological Era: A Personal Approach

9

Throughout this book, I stress the importance of the human element when it comes to technology. As we move through the eighties and into the nineties, we'll have more technology and thus more challenges. People's needs will change as they always have. Think back over the last twenty-five years; as sophisticated information technology came into our factories and offices, people restructured their values regarding work. For example, in the 1950s most people believed you took a job after high school or college and stayed with that same organization until you retired at sixty-five. This was a holdover from earlier days when the workforce wasn't very mobile. Today, people not only change jobs and organizations, they often change entire careers. I've worked for large companies, run a few businesses of my own, been a full-time college professor, and am now obviously a writer, among other things.

This chapter covers a potpourri of subjects I believe are important and relevant for the technological manager. Although we have made great strides in our understanding of management, we still have a long way to go as it pertains to humane automation.

A few years ago, I was talking with the executive vice-president of a large manufacturing firm, and we got on the subject of employee alcoholism and its partner, drug abuse. Although the following is not a direct quotation, it paraphrases what this man said about his employees:

These people create impossible home lives. They live beyond their means and have no concept of how to get ahead in the world. They're victimized and feel helpless, so they drink to forget or stick a needle in their arm to space out. If they'd fix up their home lives, they'd feel better, and then I wouldn't have these problems.

Inhumane? Uncaring? Callous? Yes, all of those. Rare? Unique? Unrepresentative? No.

When I suggested to that executive that he, personally, might be partially responsible for the condition of some of those people, he nearly came across the desk at me. It was at that moment that I became aware of something rather profound—it isn't long hours and hard work that cause executive tension. The human being, as a part of physical existence, uses his or her highly efficient cellullar machine to transport and house a nearly tireless brain. What's happening is a great inner conflict within many men and women in decision-making positions between what they want to do and what they actually do. Some of these executives feel more victimized than the people who report to them. They want to manage for human fulfillment, but they're programmed to manage for the bottom line. They create imbalances within themselves that ultimately lead to some disease: physical illness (ulcers, heart attacks, high blood pressure) and/or mental disorders (depression, worry, guilt). These conditions also can manifest in uncontrollable anger, physical violence, drug abuse (including sleeping tablets), even obesity.

I'm not trying to paint a picture of the typical manager as some kind of fiend. The majority of managers that I meet—and it's a fair number of men and women of all ages and backgrounds in a variety of large and small organizations—are loving people who put their utmost effort behind improved human relations. Still, even for those individuals, it's possible that what they do well can always be done better.

Let's look at some ways you can do your job in such a way that everyone wins. Everyone. Not just you. Not just "management." Not just the people outside of the organization who depend on it for a service or a product. Not just the workers. Everyone. Some organizations nearly achieve it and others are working toward it. I believe that we'll all get there, but I fear that there's some rough sledding ahead for some.

Ever since man first banded together into groups for more effective self-protection and collective efficiency, there have been leaders or, in a broader sense, managers—those charged with the responsibility of directing the activities of others. Although we've come a long way in learning how to "get things done with and through people" (that is, manage), we have a long way to go in helping our fellow human beings to *enjoy* their work while assisting management in satisfying organizational objectives. Many supervisors, executives, and managers view supporting the people who report to them and the satisfaction of institutional goals as separate, even unconnected, activities. This shouldn't be. Both are easily combined into a single objective that simultaneously builds both the organization and the people within it, and must be for humane management to occur.

Almost every manager—young or old, man or woman—wants to look good. Unfortunately, in some cases looking good and/or being right have become primary goals to the neglect of the more important ones, like the welfare of subordinates or even achieving some worthwhile organizational plan. If you support, love, and help those people who report to you, you can forget about looking good; it's always a byproduct.

Dr. Dale Ironson, a close friend and humanistic psychologist, easily summarized much of the "why" of management (why managers do what they do), especially the parts that rob people of their self-esteem. I asked Dale why, when we've come so far in human development, so many managers, executives, and even national leaders still operate as if other people simply don't matter. Dale's answer summed up the entire situation in one simple statement: "Because they think it works."

They think it works. Some managers still believe the way to get people to do things is to force them, make them operate out of fear: fear of rejection, fear of not getting a promotion or raise, fear of losing their job. When people direct their behavior to avoid rejection, blame, or general unpleasantness, they can never be committed to what they're doing. Their "goal" is simply not to make waves, rather than to get the job done. Not doing something is *not a clear goal*; there's nothing to shoot for, no end result in mind. The quality of work suffers and, before long, most effort is directed toward staying out of trouble with the boss rather than developing skills and a sense of self-fulfillment.

I'm not a great believer in the value of the time and money spent on laboratory rat research in quest of parallels in human behavior. Rat studies usually only make researchers more knowledgeable about rat behavior; however, there are some laboratory findings that do pertain to you and your people. One of these has to do with reward and punishment: If you reward a rat (or a person) for a particular behavior, it tends to repeat that behavior more often and more consistently. Conversely, punishment tends to restrict behavior. Punishment for laboratory rats usually consists of electrical shocks. Punishment for workers is much more complex—a frown, a verbal dressing down, probationary action, firing. But punishment for a human being, like punishment for a rat, restricts behavior. Just what the restriction becomes in human terms is often difficult to discern.

Rather than using fear or force to *control* a negative situation, let's examine some concepts that can help.

Keep such situations from arising in the first place. Always bear in mind that when you're responsible for a facility where automation is being introduced or used, the pace tends to be much faster and a single error in management may have far greater effects. For example, if you yell at Mary Ellen and then ask her to type a one-page order on her word processor and get it off to fifty suppliers before her humiliation has even begun to wane, fifty letters requesting shipments of hundreds of pairs of boobs rather than boots may be on their way to the mailroom. Mary Ellen's emotions, and yours, tend to hang around a lot longer than the minute bursts of voltage that create words, numbers, orders, accounts receivable, or inventory control inside your computer; and the effects of computer errors hang around a lot longer than either your angry outburst or Mary Ellen's hurt feelings.

The success of management in this age of computerization depends on the acceptance of six basic assumptions:

1. That love is the major guiding force and primary human need
2. That each person senses the existence of some true purpose even though he or she may be unaware of its exact identity
3. That people want to be given the power to choose
4. That all people want to experience unity, not only within themselves but with all things, including their work
5. That people's ability is inherently limitless
6. That every individual is capable of maximum performance and creativity—that is, flow

Perhaps these assumptions may seem a bit out of place in a book on technology and management, but they reflect what I've found to be true, and they appear to be the direction in which management is moving now and will move in the years to come. They also represent what an increasing number of workers view as the most important and *minimal* qualities of the workplace. As our technology becomes more complex and exceeds the ability of the average human being to comprehend either its structure or its total function, the values that are distinctly human will become more important to each of us. When the capacity of any given machine exceeds the capacity of the individuals on all *mechanical* levels (quality, quantity, and amount of work performed), how an individual *feels* becomes critical. If ultimately the *only* quality the employee sees to his/her function as an individual beyond that of the machine is "I feel," management must be able to recognize and utilize this fantastic, uniquely human resource.

These concepts will work in a large manufacturing company, a hospital, a gas station, a government agency, a restaurant, even the military. The size of the management unit isn't important. The age of the people isn't an issue. Educational level doesn't matter. The only thing that matters is a true sensitivity that comes from love. It's that simple; but love and concern for others must begin with love itself.

The Concept of Love

I use the word *love*, not to make you uncomfortable or because I'm a poet or leftover Flower Child of the sixties. (I'm neither.) I use the word because I'm talking about the fundamental unit of feeling that *includes* caring, concern, empathy, and all the other intermediate (and sometimes watered down) emotions we business people more easily bandy about. If simply reading the word in a management text makes the majority of us uncomfortable, you can imagine how remote its actual application is in the American workplace. Genuine love among executives, managers, and workers is what many believe gives the Japanese the competitive advantage. Love is not emotional claptrap; it makes good business sense.

I realize this may be a difficult chapter for many because, like me, you were taught a standard of management where emotions in any form were considered detrimental to production. But although scientific management techniques are extremely useful and can help you do your job more effectively, most of us need to concentrate first on the very basics of management—the people. Love is the power that fuses a working unit, an entire organization, a nation, even the world. Many times managers find love a difficult concept to deal with because there are so many definitions. Obviously if you're a female manager overseeing a crew of men of the "breath and britches" variety, you're bound to be reluctant to refer to your love for them. Similarly, male managers who feel certain female employees are already overly solicitous would certainly hesitate to introduce love into their conversations. However, it may not be necessary to say the word at all; if your feelings are genuine, they'll invariably be conveyed in the proper way. There's no way to confuse the composite, concerned, caring love we're talking about with mere sexuality. The only way that message is received is if that's the message you send. Consequently, you must be aware of your own feelings before you can convey them successfully to others. Love simply means you want your people to have the things they want for themselves; it doesn't necessarily require that *you* provide it. Say one of your subordinates wants to be paid $3000 a week and he is now making $300. If you love him, you recognize the validity of his desire *for him*, but you feel no obligation to provide it if it runs counter to your own beliefs and/or abilities.

Some people think introducing love invariably results in either management nihilism or true communal management. That's highly unlikely. Very little gets accomplished when a committee or work group is left without good, helpful, loving guidance. Work groups *want* such assistance. To be sure, the support and guidance you provide as a manager is often quite minimal when your directives are based on love and concern for your people, but the response is always maximal.

If you want to change the way you function as a manager, you must start at the beginning. The beginning is easy; first love yourself—truly, totally, unreservedly. Once you've done that, the rest is a snap.

The Concept of True Nature and Purpose

How many times have you said or done something and then immediately thought, "That's not like me." When you become aware of this apparent contradiction in behavior, you actually make a rather phenomenal discovery about yourself: You give yourself very definite clues about how you want to be. And you immediately recognize that uncomfortable feeling that comes from operating counter to this inner standard—your true nature.

Many of us are victims to one degree or another of what Wayne Dyer (in his book *Your Erroneous Zones*, Thomas Y. Crowell, 1976) calls "musterbations." You "must" not have more than one cocktail during a business lunch. You "must" answer an incoming letter at the same organizational level as the sender. You "must" wear clothes of a certain style. And so on. Organizations in general prescribe a code of etiquette to which each subordinate structure adds its own unique set of musts and shoulds.

Most of this code of what should or must go on is totally made up. A certain group thinks it works. Sometimes it does; a lot of the time it doesn't. What happens if your made-up list of musts and shoulds runs counter to that of your workers? When people are asked to operate counter to their true nature, imbalances occur that interfere with their productivity. If these imbalances continue, they can cause mental distress and physical illness. Many people get fired for being ineffective in their jobs; probably at least some of their lack of effectiveness stems from the fact that they are consistently being asked to run counter to their true nature. Unfortunately, defining a person's true nature, like love, is easier said than done because it's a highly individualistic feeling rather than a measurable skill. However, it is relatively easy to discover some of the characteristics that describe a person's true nature and it doesn't take a battery of tests to do it.

We spend a major part of our waking hours at our job, traveling to and from it and just thinking about it. For most people, especially managers and executives, it's probably the one item that occupies most of their thoughts. We may love our family more than our job, but we probably think more about the job than the family. Suppose you (or one of your people) now hold a job that is counter to an overall true nature or purpose. What do you think happens?

What seems to happen is best described as a misalignment. People feel manipulated and out of control, out of phase or alignment with what they want to be. The longer the misalignment continues, the more people feel they no longer control their own destiny. Such people are usually inefficient—their "heart isn't in their work." It's usually fairly easy to spot such people. Perhaps some even work for you. Or you may be one yourself. When people are misaligned for a long time, they begin feeling irritable and depressed; this separation can lead to drug and alcohol abuse. The extreme case of maximum misalignment is suicide and, as we know, all too often unrewarding careers are a causative factor in self-destruction.

One of a manager's tasks is to help people discover their life's work as it fits into the entire picture of their true nature and purpose. This may mean having the self-confidence (self-love) to let some of your best subordinates go on to other careers with your blessing. It's the people who are of primary importance, not the structure. If you care about the people, the structure will always be strong.

The Concept of Choice

The third concept that simplifies management in our high-tech era is an awareness of choice as an effective tool for creating a strong management/worker bond.

Managers are often well-versed in decision making, but know little about choice. The major difference is that decision making is passive (it's defined most simply as making up one's mind about one thing or another); whereas choice is an active and creative process. By making choice an active part of your organization, you help people learn they can choose their feelings, the state of their health, and their careers, as well as the most productive way to do their job for you.

For many in the working world, their present career level results from happenstance. They took a job at a local factory or in a small store because they honestly believed it was the only thing open to them at the time. To them, it was not a choice, it was a reaction to present conditions. "What choice did I have?" "What else could I do?" As life progresses, they stay in that first job, receiving raises and promotions, but without ever really *choosing* to be there. They respond to stimuli in terms of finding a rapid solution to what they perceive as an immediate problem rather than creative opportunity; they act in haste with many repenting at their leisure. Unfortunately, many times managers fully support this limiting view in their subordinates. "Jack's a good worker as long as I tell him exactly what to do." "Harry will never be anything but a good programmer."

Using choice in a working environment means managers and subordinates create choices about what they want regardless of whether or not they think all those choices are possible. Rather than saying, "This is what needs to be done and this is how we're going to do it," try "This is what needs to be done. How do you think we should do it?" At first it may seem like this takes much longer; that's because workers tend to be stunned by management's willingness to let them participate in the design of their work, to say nothing of the love/concern such willingness implies. However, once the novelty of humane treatment becomes an accepted fact, your workforce will become consistently more efficient and creative.

The Concept of Unity

Many ancient and modern philosophers and scientists speak of the universe as totally integrated: that all physical and nonphysical entities are locked and integrated into a whole. Out of this comes the concept of holism, a theory maintaining that reality is composed of unified bits and pieces whose combined form exceeds the sum of the parts. It's similar to synergy, which was a faddish management term in the sixties and seventies. Like holism, synergy said that one and one makes three. The problem in most organizations is that one and one usually amounts to zero or less because people, groups, departments, and entire organizations battle against each other. Even competition should never be viewed as the enemy—a competitive organization is simply someone in the same business as you are, in many ways the very reason you choose to excel. In other words, how good you are is often because of the quality of your competition.

Holistic management means that every aspect involving people has the concept of unity attached to it. It starts with the individual. A person can't be whole, be one, if parts of his or her life aren't aligned. Self-love, again, is the starting point, the place of initial focus. Holism evolving from the personal starting point of self-love means that all individuals within the smallest work unit see themselves as a whole—bonded together for mutual support, led by another aligned individual called the supervisor, and united for some common goal. The goal may be to produce a ¾-inch-long bolt with a minimum number of defects or to find a cure for cancer. As there is nobility in all work that feels right for the person doing it, so there is nobility in any goal deemed worthy of attainment by any work unit regardless of size or complexity.

The Concept of Limitlessness

People are noble. They are divine. They're also limitless; what limitations exist are those we make in the mind. Shakespeare said that "there is nothing either good or bad, but thinking makes it so," and the Bible says that "as a man thinks in his heart, so he is" (Proverbs 23:7). The basic

114

underlying premise for the concept of limitlessness is based on the fact that it's possible to attain desirable goals by (1) making proper choices about the goals, (2) having people see what they want as if it's already accomplished, and (3) by helping people believe they can have what they want.

Too many managers spend far too much time concentrating on problems and limitations and the reasons why they and their people can't get things done. Concentrating on limitations only creates more limitations.

The Concept of Flow and Maximum Creativity

One of the current problems with creativity is that much of our natural ability is systematically schooled out of us. A large part of what we learn as youngsters is what we can't do; we're often taught the nature of our limitations rather than our limitlessness. Every person is capable of superhuman energy that can be creatively channelled. This energy is variously called "peaking," "maximum performance," or "flow." All of us experience flow at some point in our lives; some people experience it continuously. When we feel flow, everything seems right; there's an overall sense of total cooperation.

Recognizing flow is important in order to learn to use it. Flow invariably occurs when there's a real commitment to a task at hand and when we feel that the task will enrich us. Managers can develop flow with their subordinates by strongly focusing on the individual and group goals and objectives. People who experience flow in their work recognize immediately those things that are or are not consistent with the process and the goal; they're happy and feel the work itself is effortless. So great is the effect of flow that many who experience it claim their efforts are aided by forces they can neither understand nor describe, but are nonetheless real.

Detecting Imbalance

It's an interesting hypothesis that there must always be reasons why things go wrong. I don't mean reasons in the way that we normally think of them. For example, a powdered breakfast food called Gorilla's Milk flopped horribly because of its name and because Pillsbury's Instant Breakfast already had a strong hold on the market. The name and market considerations are reasons of perceptual reality—they reflect conditions that anyone can see and analyze. The kind of reasons I'm talking about go beyond our normal business way of figuring things out. What I'm talking about is most closely described by the word "intuition," those reasons more commonly felt than verbalized or tabulated. Intuition is defined as the process of knowing something without the aid of a rational thinking process; and it does seem that women are better at it than men. This tendency may be explained by the fact that in the past we tended to rear our daughters to be more sensitive, whereas our sons were counseled to think logically and not be misled by their feelings. It is acknowledged, however, that men and women are innately intuitively equal and anyone can regain the skill with practice.

Some of the most successful managers in this country admit that they make their best decisions intuitively. It's their intuition that tells them something's wrong. All of us can detect imbalances between our intuitive and learned responses through a logical process, but most of us simply recognize it as simply not feeling right about some goal or task. Managers can choose to bypass those feelings, but they should be able to recognize them. Unfortunately, modern managers learn very early in their careers to place a high priority on views supported by lots of good, concrete reasons. Computer printouts, mathematical techniques, surveys, facts, even opinions of groups are considered appropriate means of authentication. Feelings, emotions, and intuition are often cited as frivolous, when, in fact, they should rank at least equally with the more classical data. As we discover more about such abilities as precognition (knowing about an outcome before it occurs), effective managers of the future will indeed tap into their extrasensory powers as well as those of their subordinates to aid in overall decision making. As electro-mechanical technology increases, it's naive for any manager to believe that the abilities of the human being will remain static. Perhaps the idea of trusting your intuition seems archaic with all that sophisticated automation around you and more on the way; but as I said before, it's how you and your people think and feel that makes you and them different from, and in many ways superior to, these marvelous machines. Now that the computer can do the mundane and most superficial mental functions, your and your employees are free to explore the hitherto unknown corners of your minds. Not only is it fun and exciting, it adds a whole new dimension to your organization.

Dealing with Problem People

My six concepts won't work on 2 to 7 percent of the people regardless of the situation and the manager. This frustrates some managers because they believe they must be effective 100 percent of the time. That's a lofty goal to strive for, but the truth is that some people simply won't respond. But before giving up, it's important to (1) find out if that person recognizes what they're feeling and doing, and (2) help that person make the proper choices about what they *want* to feel and do if their current feelings aren't acceptable to them. If you view management as your responsibility to contribute to the betterment of your people, it's easy for you to become involved in this process. However, there will be those who simply don't respond no matter what you do. The reasons may rest entirely with them, or you may be ineffective in dealing with them. It really doesn't matter. If you see little or no change, seek help from other sources or find some other place for that person to work, even if it means firing him or her.

Don't evade the issue of problem people. In all areas of management, but particularly in our computerized workplace of high-speed production and output, one disgruntled employee can have a tremendous negative effect, not only on your product, but also on his or her coworkers in a very short period of time. By choosing not to confront the issue, you subject yourself, the problem worker, and your entire workforce to an inferior standard of employment. Managers are hired to *fix* things that go wrong in addition to keeping them from going wrong. Too often managers think that acknowledging the existence of a problem employee reflects negatively on them, particularly if they hired that person. It doesn't unless you choose to ignore it.

What Is Power?

The real meaning of power has been lost in a large sense in the business world. To many, power is might, force, control over others. That's not power at all—that's a *loss of power.* The word *power* comes from an ancient French verb, *poeir,* meaning to be able. True power is personal and represents the *ability to be in control of yourself.* It represents the ability to choose how to react to situations—from those that involve you intimately (being fired, going through a divorce, experiencing a loss of income) to those that barely involve you at all (the weather in Rome, the wild gerbil population in Mongolia).

Although it's not a hard and fast rule, people seem to seek power over others as they lose it in themselves. In the twentieth century, the individual who wielded the greatest degree of power over others was also the individual who had little or no personal power—a man who took his own life in a contaminated bunker within a city that was to be a living symbol of his empire—Adolf Hitler.

Authority is another concept often linked to power. Many people agree with the dictionary that authority represents the "right to command." However, authority is something that is *given* to an individual by those over whom he or she exerts influence. Authority is delegated and consequently can be removed. It is a gift from one's subordinates, not a privilege of rank. Authoritarian managers who fail to recognize this find their subordinates simply don't obey them. Either they ignore such a person, openly rebel against his or her authority, or remove themselves from such an environment—first by failing to show up for work regularly (tardiness and/or absenteeism) and then by resigning. I hear hundreds of managers complain about turnover in their organizations; the majority blame the workers. I've only heard one or two supervisors wonder whether it might be something in themselves that causes the problem. No, employees don't leave for higher pay and better benefits. People don't normally quit for those reasons, even though finding a "better-paying job" is often cited in the classic exit interview because that's a reason many managers can accept. If your subordinates resign because your idea of authority impresses them as tyrannical despotism created by your own lack of self-confidence and self-love, it's safe to assume they would most likely opt to soothe your fragile ego with references to some "better-paying job" rather than risk the consequences of the truth. If you're a truly powerful individual, such posturing isn't necessary; that is, subordinates can quit, be fired, or be hired and it has *no* effect on how you feel about yourself as a manager and as a person.

How Managers Create Problems

Let's briefly discuss the two areas that create the most problems for manager: lying and the need to be right.

At some point, all parents tell their children not to lie. Initially, children accept this advice, but usually only until they discover that everybody lies, including parents. First, they figure out that lying's okay under certain circumstances; white lies are usually acceptable, telling someone that a new dress looks great when indeed it looks atrocious is considered good manners. If lying to make others look good is acceptable, then, by inference, lying to make ourselves look good is also condoned.

Some managers make a personal effort to be truthful, whereas others hardly seem able to distinguish between lying and telling the truth. The reasons for lying aren't important; the consequences of lying, however, can be disastrous, especially if it becomes a habit.

In 1926, Leonarde Keeler developed the first polygraph, which detects when a person is lying by sensing changes in breathing and pulse rate. Lying produces such an extreme effect physiologically that it could be detected by relatively unsophisticated devices over half a century ago! Imagine the long-term effects of lying on the human body. Lying isn't only wrong, it's self-destructive. Because of these extreme effects, lying is also unnatural.

Lying has a closely allied counterpart: the need (for managers) to be right, the sin of self-justification. Many people seem afraid to say, "I was wrong," or "I made a mistake." That's because the brutal fact is that being wrong in most organizations usually means reprimand or termination. Consequently, an inordinate amount of time and effort is spent protecting oneself with only one objective in mind—that of being right. You do it; your subordinates do it.

How did such a nonproductive practice get started? Some anthropologists and social scientists suggest that because prehistoric man was involved in a life-and-death situation, making accurate predictions (that is, being right) about what to eat and where to live meant survival. Consequently, the people who most accurately forecast the outcome of a particular situation were elevated to positions of authority.

We still revere such individuals today, especially when predictions come true in the face of what appears to be strong evidence to the contrary. Most Americans remember Joe Namath predicting the New York Jets would beat the Colts in the first AFL-NFL Superbowl, and the seemingly outrageous claim by Muhammad Ali (then Cassius Clay) that he would beat Sonny Liston in the ring. Being right carries its own mystique. It *implies* power. However, it is *not* power.

The connection we make between being right and power is one that we make in our minds; and it can just as easily be broken there. In most cases, there is no value to being right except that which we invent. Being right doesn't make anyone better or guarantee their performance or productivity; but if it's important to you, it will also be important to your people and a waste of time.

Becoming an Aligned Manager

Throughout our discussion of the concepts (love, purpose, choice, unity, limitlessness, and flow) and problems (imbalance, problem people, power, authority, lying, and being right) inherent in humane management, we refer to being aligned, to feeling good about yourself, on numerous occasions. However, how do you know if you're aligned in your managerial philosophy? Part of becoming aligned simply means beginning to be aware of your true nature and purpose. As you do this, you experience flow, your thinking becomes clearer, and you truly feel that everything is cooperating with you (unity).

Becoming aligned means you pay attention to yourself, your feelings, and what you want. Because you spend so much time on the job, the first thing you must evaluate is how you feel about your job. You can't help others learn to enjoy themselves and their work if you don't share those feelings. Or, as Shakespeare so aptly put it, "To thine own self be true." If you truly believe what you're doing is the right work for you, you automatically transmit that in the form of love, purpose, choice, unity, limitlessness, and flow to all those around you. If you honestly feel your present job isn't right for you, by all means heed that feeling. People often don't want to end a career that may represent a major part of their lives because they feel they've made too great an investment to change. They may cite personal status, seniority, pension benefits, and the like as the reasons; but these are only made up and probably aren't important at all. If you spend a large portion of your work helping and guiding others, you may now need to guide yourself in response to how you feel your life is going. You may find that after finally arriving at a lofty executive pinnacle at Gigantic Industries, your true purpose is better served by starting your own business, becoming a social worker, or beginning an entirely new career. Regardless of how successful others may consider you, if you aren't totally at peace (aligned) with your work, you'll never be truly happy or work to your full capacity.

There's a Buddhist philosophy of "right livelihood" that maintains that when one discovers his or her life's work, one major segment of the alignment process occurs. At that point, work ceases to be work; it becomes play, and the former distinction between work and recreation disappears. It's not difficult to see the advantages of working with and for such a person, is it?

There. We made it through one of the toughest chapters. It's always a lot easier to read about things we can do to help or change our subordinates rather than those things that necessitate change in ourselves. This is especially difficult when we're dealing with something as nebulous as emotions; but once you understand your feelings and how to change them, you can use them to add new dimensions to your managerial skills. Now let's look at some ways you can do this.

Understanding and Helping Your Subordinates

10

As a manager, you already know that your personal success depends directly on how efficiently and effectively your subordinates function. The more you give them what they want, the more you receive in return. They can make you look great; they can make you look terrible. It all starts with you.

The Self-Created Reality

If you take all of the concepts and problems described in the last chapter and accept them or reject them, you're left with your own highly personal, self-created managerial reality. For example, if you say "that love stuff is a bunch of hogwash" or "I don't have to be right, I just hate being wrong!" your idea of how you function is not the same as someone who says, "It seems a little weird, but I think I'll try loving old Ken instead of being mad at him all the time," or "Maybe being right *is* too important to me." If both these individuals manage the same group of subordinates, it's obvious that how they view those people and their relationship to them is quite different. Although this seems readily apparent, it's surprising how difficult it is for many managers to accept the fact that *no one* sees or does things the same way they do. Everyone sees and does things in his or her own way; each one of us creates our own reality that is very real to us, and very unique. Consequently, we need to understand this concept of personally created reality to appreciate how we and others operate. Let's see how it works.

The chart that follows compares the three most common views people have of their realities; that is, how they view themselves in terms of how they view others. By using this chart, you can see how your self-view affects/interacts with the self-view of those around you. For example, if you have positive feelings about your reality and see your subordinates' feelings as equally positive, the two of you create a reality far different from the one created if you perceive your subordinates negatively or vice versa.

Because many people direct their attention outside their lives in terms of their relationships, finances, and careers, they believe things happen *to* them. Take the case of those who get fired. They invariably say, "I got fired," as if someone arbitrarily took their job from them. As you know, few people "get fired"—they get *themselves* fired because of incompetence, lack of work, or personality differences. Essentially, most people create situations that result in their release from employment. The individual who gets fired actually co-creates the entire drama with others from the beginning to the end. It's easier, though, to blame outside influences. People say it makes them feel better. Maybe it does; however, it also denies what the situation was and is and removes their sense of being in control of their lives.

In your day-to-day existence, you deal with three seemingly nonphysical items: thoughts, feelings, and intuitions. For all their seeming lack of a physical structure or form, they're much more important to you and others around you than anything that has weight or occupies space. They're what make you you; they're the tools you use to build your reality. None of them are inherent in that automated environment where you and your people work; yet they affect every single thing you do. By fully grasping the part that those abilities play in your multiple managerial roles, you can literally change negative situations/realities (a fear of computerization, anti-computer feelings resulting from an inadequate system) into positive ones.

How Thoughts Influence Your Relationship
with Your Subordinates

A thought is a thing, but also the process the mind uses to know something. We have thoughts continuously. We produce some spontaneously; others we work out over a period of time. You drive to work and suddenly remember a nine o'clock meeting with your boss. Where did that thought come from? The clock on the bank you passed? The radio an-

 Other View \ Self-View	Positive	Neutral	Negative
Positive	(+,+) Aligned and centered Personally balanced Love for self and others At peace with the world On a path to wisdom and understanding Holistic—one with universe	(0,+) Things generally okay "People are nice, but generally better than I am." May only be a transitional phase to (+,+)	(−,+) Frustration Feelings of inferiority "The world is lovely but beyond my reach." "I wish I could be someone else."
Neutral	(+,0) "I'm great but the world needs help." "Maybe I can help others to improve." Hope and optimism may be present.	(0,0) "Why try?" World appears random with little progress. "I'm average in an average world." Consistent, repetitive lifestyle.	(−,0) No self-responsibility View of self as either victim or martyr Change is difficult to bring about Fear of self in a world that is arbitrary
Negative	(+,−) May lead to feelings of supremacy in a world of fools and underlings View of self as a "monarch" Others to be distrusted, feared, manipulated "I'll get mine first. To hell with the weak."	(0,−) "Watch out!" "The world will get you if you're not careful." Things pretty hopeless Life seen as constant battle for survival Muddling through, usually ineffectively	(−,−) Out of control, lost Utter despair Possible insanity, suicide, violence Hopelessness and powerlessness

nouncer's reference to someone's boss? The stimulus may have no conscious connection to your thought at all. All you know is that *you* produced the thought; you made it up. Because of that, you can change your thoughts in a moment. If you're thinking about making love, you can instantly switch to figuring out how you're going to pay for your new car. You can play out panorama and melodrama, solve problems, fantasize, remember, imagine, project, create, and erase all in a second's time. Our thoughts are uniquely our own.

Initially, this concept may seem threatening, particularly if you harbor some nasty thought—like strangling your boss—but it needn't be. If you think about strangling your boss, what can you say about the nature of that thought? You might say it has nothing to do with you at all; that is, "The Devil made me think it." Or you might say, "It's my own thought and I'm a rotten person for creating it." The third choice requires an understanding of, and belief in, yourself as a person who intuitively recognizes his or her true nature and any imbalance with it. "I created the thought because I need it. What does it teach me about myself and how I feel?" These are three possible origins and reactions to the same thought. Which one do you prefer? Which one is more real to you?

Your thoughts are part of your inner reality and as such become highly textured or flavored by your perception. Once you have a belief, whatever it is, you experience the "truth" to reinforce that belief. If several of your subordinates believe management is incompetent, they'll find evidence to support that belief in almost everything you do. If their perception of you and other managers as incompetent bunglers is strong enough, they can actually become unable to recognize any evidence of managerial competency.

I was a consultant to a small business in which the employees believed the owners were only in business for the money. Because the employees had to support their "the owners-don't-give-a-damn-about-us-only-about-money" belief, they created negative situations to reinforce their collective reality. The owners, who actually held quite a positive view of their people but had difficulty expressing it, were initially baffled by the behavior, but soon began operating in a fashion directly supporting the drama. They began to function under an "*employees*-don't-give-a-damn" belief. It became so complicated that even when we made significant positive changes for the employees—more vacation time and higher pay—the employees saw this as an act of guilt or, at best, institutional bribery to get them to work harder. The owners responded to what they considered their employees' ingratitude with the belief that the employees didn't care about them or their work at all; all the employees cared about was money! Back to square one.

All managers experience similar unproductive situations ("If management really cared, they wouldn't replace people with computers"), and your task is identical to mine as consultant to the emotion-torn business: You must get each faction to realize how their individual thoughts co-create this situation that no one likes. Encourage each party to examine their basic belief and make changes.

Another example is a client who's greatly hampered in his business because he believes "good help is hard to find." To him, "good help" means someone who

1. Works at the minimum wage and expects no benefits.
2. Never misses a moment's work.
3. Doesn't complain about anything.
4. Stays on the job forever.
5. Demonstrates loyalty to the point of fanaticism.

As you might suspect, he has a turnover problem. Because of his beliefs, he hires people who help him prove himself right, the exact opposite of what he says he wants. He hires people who are likely to quit, and he produces conditions that help bring it about. He sets it up that way; it's his SFP although he's not consciously aware of it.

In these two cases, the solutions come from a change in people's thoughts. If the person with the turnover problem changes his belief to one that sees people as human beings first and employees who want to enjoy their work second, he no longer needs to prove himself right. He releases himself from a belief system that is quite limiting, harms his business, and restricts his personal growth.

I'm certainly not advocating anything like corporate brainwashing, where everyone is encouraged to think along identical lines. ("We all love our word processor, don't we?") If we could all produce the same thoughts and hold identical beliefs, life would be dull and little growth would occur. Organizational uniformity is potential organizational suicide. What I want managers to strive for is free individual expression of ideas, beliefs, and theories, but not as inviolate, unchangeable entities. Thoughts should be examined to determine whether or not that idea is *useful* to its creator and the work unit. That's the major test, the utility of an idea or a belief. If it's not a useful idea to you or your people, regardless of the reasons, get rid of it.

Getting rid of negative ideas seems like a simple thing, doesn't it? Why would people want to keep something around that's not working for them? Sometimes old ideas and beliefs are like old shoes; they no longer fit or function well, but they're familiar. Such reluctance to give up old ideas is particularly strong when automation occurs. When your bookkeepers and stenographers compare their terminals and word processors to their familiar calculators and typewriters, if they're the least bit apprehensive they may want to cling to some old (and now inappropriate) ideas for security. ("I don't want to move my desk." "I don't want to do the invoices in batches like that.")

Because eliminating or changing negative thoughts can be difficult, it's often helpful to use visualization techniques. Some managers believe that using such aids means they're "not smart enough" to get rid of the idea(s) logically. It's not that at all. By putting the idea in a completely different form and setting, it's often possible to do the job more quickly. Let's look at two different techniques and how to use them.

Getting Rid of Negative Beliefs
About Specific Individuals

The first technique is for handling a belief you have about a specific person. When you produce a belief (thought) within yourself, you give it existence, power, and form. Thoughts aren't ethereal, fleeting wisps of consciousness that last only for milliseconds and then disappear. Thoughts have a physical quality about them and are capable of producing physical changes. Thought produces form. *It's not the other way around.* As we saw in our examples, if you have a belief about someone, you supply psychic ammunition to that belief and person, and actually reinforce your belief within the individual. You create what you hold as true. If you believe someone has a quality about them you want to change—a careless programmer, for example—first recognize that you have that belief. After you recognize the belief, accept it. Realize that you produced it and *no one else.* You may have adopted someone else's ideas, but you created the belief for yourself and gave it power. Accepting a belief as your creation is critical because it gives you the awareness that *only* you can change it. After you recognize and accept the belief, you're ready to produce the change.

Suppose you have a subordinate you believe is too nervous to use your expensive new computer. Become aware of the belief and the fact that you created it; accept it without blame or censorship. Visualize all your beliefs about nervous behavior. For example, imagine your subordinate doing something totally ludicrous at the terminal, like wearing the buttons off the keyboard with her nervous fingerings.

Remember the biblical admonition to pluck out one's eye if it's offensive? The same visual analogy works well with nonproductive beliefs. See the belief as a diseased tree in a forest; the forest represents other positive beliefs you have about the individual. Mentally, pluck out that tree and discard it. Rip it out by its roots and throw it away.

You can create your own method of getting rid of unwanted beliefs if you don't like trees. However, it's important to use some form of visualization that expresses the invasive nature of any belief. You want to remove the entire belief, not just the part you can see.

Once you remove the belief and discard it, fill the "hole" that you have created with the belief you want. See your employee as more energetic, capable of greater output with some special guidance. If you can't think of anything with which to replace the undesired thought, simply fill the cavity with peace. See peace in any shape that you want: The popular form of a dove or olive branch is fine, but any image that means peace to you will work.

You are like a surgeon removing a specific growth. If you discover that the growth returns (that you are re-creating the thought), you may want to remove it again. If it reappears again, the basic concepts of love, purpose, choice, and so on are not being fulfilled. Either you or your subordinate, or both of you, wish to perpetuate the belief. At this point, you must take the time to discuss your beliefs thoroughly with each other to determine whether change or termination is the most sensitive and caring way to resolve the problem.

Dealing with Faulty Generalized Beliefs

The second technique for across-the-board generalizations like "the problem in all labor-management disputes rests with the union (or with management)" or "women employees are better than men" begins with the same awareness, acceptance, and no-blame attitude used above.

This time, see the belief in some small form that you pack into a suitcase that has no identification. Imagine closing the suitcase and driving to your nearest bus terminal, railroad station, or airport—any place that has rental lockers. Find a locker, place the suitcase in the locker, toss the key into a river, and walk away. Never return to claim your bag. Forget where you left it.

Using Your Thoughts
to Influence Your Subordinates

These are not managerial parlor games. You can consistently help your subordinates through your own thoughts alone. Remember: This is not power to manipulate people to do your will. You can only supply energy to move people in a direction they want to go. If you attempt to exert your will over someone—whether by verbal and open commands, veiled threats, or even thoughts, you only produce negative effects in yourself.

If one of your subordinates is an alcoholic and you feel powerless to help that person in a conscious way, simply project your thoughts about that person. See his alcoholism as a temporary situation that can be corrected. You can help; but if you see him as a hopeless drunk who will only get worse, you provide psychic encouragement for this negative condition. Many managers and counselors who fail to generate appropriate beliefs about people they say they want to help wonder why they're not more effective. Often it's because they see the person as a problem rather than as the potentially happy, creative individual he or she wants to be. Your thoughts are important because they establish reality—they create it in a conscious sense—and co-create the reality of others.

The action isn't the person. The person isn't the thought. You're not just the collective sum of your experiences. As soon as you start playing "he is..." or "I am..." or any of those games that label people, you immediately limit your thinking. You restrict yourself and others. You limit creativity.

Supervisors, managers, executives, and business owners need a more open, positive, and directed way of thinking about themselves and about subordinates in this complex computerized business world. This isn't just the power of positive thinking, although there's nothing terribly wrong with seeing the beauty in everything or with always wanting things to turn out the right way for you. However, there's a tendency to deny or ignore the original condition like a strong, personal dislike for a subordinate, or to gloss over it as unimportant. Be aware of your thoughts, admit them—after all, you made them. There's nothing wrong with them, and since you created them, you can change them.

Your Feelings Affect Your Subordinates

I have no idea how many feelings we have, maybe even millions. Most people say they want feelings like love, happiness, satisfaction, security, awe, bliss, peace, and don't want those like jealousy, greed, hatred, anger, frustration. Like thoughts, you generate feelings; they don't float into your office on some kind of divine wind (kamikaze) and cling to you like an airborne parasite. You create them and so do your subordinates. Unfortunately, after years of conditioning, many people think their feelings are automatic.

We forget that we each produce our own feelings even though we all knew this as children. Remember skinning your knee and waiting until you got home to cry? Many of us still do that, except the adult process is more sophisticated.

It's vitally important to recognize your feelings as your creation. It's misleading and a bit dangerous to your humane development to make a statement such as, "My office manager makes me furious." You make yourself furious. You generate the fury because that's what you taught

128

yourself to do. In fact, you may have so conditioned yourself to be furious when you see your office manager that it's become a habit as strong as cigarette smoking and sometimes harder to break.

Controlling feelings doesn't mean using programs to train individuals or groups to produce those feelings the programmers deem desirable. In the book *1984* by George Orwell (Harcourt, Brace & Co., Inc., 1949), audiences who saw the face of Big Brother in a movie theater were expected to generate love, a sense of belonging, excitement, security, rapture, and well-being. Any attempts to reprogram yourself or your people, even with the entire realm of positive feelings, only limits spontaneity, and that limits creativity. What is important, as in the case of thoughts, is awareness.

Suppose you have a subordinate you don't like. It's not important *why* you dislike that person. (There actually may be a slight danger in figuring out the *why* because that may only reinforce the basic premise that you dislike him or her.) After making yourself aware of the feeling of dislike and accepting your personal responsibility for producing it, ask yourself, "Is this feeling what I want?" If it isn't—that is, you don't want to dislike the person—change. You *can* change your entire feeling, but only if that's *what you want*. If you're unclear about what you want in terms of feelings, yield to your intuition, your inner judgment.

If your feeling of dislike is tied up directly with a specific act—like an individual's consistently being late—you can also change how you feel about the action. "He always gets his work done and does it well, even though he's always ten minutes late every morning" instead of "His lateness drives me crazy!" It can be helpful to talk with your subordinate, but stay away from that meaningless question so many managers ask—"Why do you do it?" Chances are the subordinate will only make up a reason. The real answer to "Why do you do . . . ?" is always "Because I want to." Now let's face it, no one in their right mind is going to tell the boss they do something the boss doesn't like because they want to. Bosses don't like to hear that, even though the only reason bosses do things is because *they* want to. An open and honest approach works much better: "Jerry, over the last month you've been more than ten minutes late ten days out of twenty-two. Punctuality is important for me to run this unit the way I want, so I want you to come to work on time. How do you feel about this?" This approach not only begins a discussion that may bring about the change you want, it also shows your subordinate that you care about his feelings too.

One of the big issues today is job security. Everyone wants to feel secure. Some people believe a job *gives* them security. A few people may go so far as to see a job *as* security. A job is a job. Security is security. A job is a thing, an activity performed in exchange for payment. Security is a feeling of freedom from risk, danger, doubt, or anxiety. There is no connection between the security and a job unless we make one.

Because security is a feeling, we can choose to feel secure in any environment. In 1966, I chose to go to Vietnam. At the time, many of my friends and colleagues thought I was either totally insane or a super hawk/paid killer. I was neither. Going to Vietnam was a conscious choice I made to learn several lessons, among them the nature of security. My lesson from Vietnam: You make your own security. You can be surrounded by numerous threats upon your very life and limb and choose how you want to feel. I'm not saying I didn't experience fear, anger, frustration, loneliness, yearning—I did; but I also experienced the true security of knowing I, alone, was responsible for those feelings.

Sometimes we use feelings as a test. We allow our true feelings to come through and sense the feelings of others in any given situation. Keep in mind that you have both true feelings and manufactured feelings. True feelings are a part of your true, aligned inner self—the real you, if you will; manufactured feelings result from training. Suppose you wear a new outfit to work and someone tells you it looks hideous. Most people automatically generate an "angry" feeling. Some may be delighted because normally everyone ignores them, and some accept the information strictly as unemotional data they may or may not choose to consider. In the real sense, what you wear has little relevance to your overall, multidimensional, eternal self. Clothes don't make the man. How the man feels about his clothes does.

Once you begin opening your inner senses, you can measure your feelings and others in somewhat the same way you compare an actual expenditure to a budgeted expense: You can see what your reality produces versus your inner standard. The next time you attend a small meeting, see if you can become aware of the emotional essence of the group. If you're like I am, you can feel the change as individuals contribute their feelings about what is happening and how they perceive it. As you gain more skill, you can even sort out individual feelings from those of the group.

One final note about feelings: Have you ever experienced a situation in which you didn't produce a feeling you expected to produce? Maybe your boss threatened to fire you and, instead of creating anxiety, you produced feelings of joy. Those were probably your true feelings coming through rather than manufactured ones. Pay attention to them!

Using Your Intuitions
and Those of Your Subordinates

Intuitions are often defined as ideas that are *made known* to the mind; they seem to come from beyond us. Many people deny intuitive thought. They have been educated that this kind of magic is not real; but many believe intuitions are a manager's greatest asset.

So often, though, intuition is stifled. In my first professional job, my boss asked me for reasons to support my recommendations for solving a problem. I told him my ideas were the result of how I felt about it. He proceeded to give me quite a lecture on the right logical, directed thought process versus the wrong intuitive way of arriving at conclusions. His gentle but firm lecture set standards that persisted for over fifteen years, standards I had to dismember totally later on when I discovered that his views were incorrect and misleading. It wasn't that he was trying to mislead me; he was being as helpful as he could. He simply didn't know that there was another side of things.

A series of experiments were conducted by several research groups comparing "good" executives and "poor" ones. These men and women were judged good or poor based upon such measurable quantities as successful new product/service introduction, low turnover, cost reduction and/or profit improvement. Essentially, their past decisions and attitudes were examined and they were divided into two groups labeled "generally effective" and "generally ineffective." One of the tests used a standard ESP card deck whose cards have symbols like stars, squares, circles, which the subjects try to guess. The effective group of managers scored significantly higher on ESP potential than the ineffective group.

If you have no real direct experience with your intuitions, try this simple experiment. Think of a minor conflict you're experiencing and two or three alternative solutions. This can be personal (whether to fix the old car or buy a new one) or professional (whether to buy a new computer or hire a new person).

Relax in a quiet area where you won't be disturbed. Sit down (or better yet, lie down), close your eyes, and slowly take three deep breaths. Clear your mind of all the conscious clutter. When you're relaxed—this may take a minute or two—think of one of the alternatives (fix the old car) and ask for a yes or no answer relative to it. Your answer may not come through as the words "yes" or "no" emblazoned on the back of your eyelids, although some people do generate answers this way. You may experience it as symbols, colors, sounds, or sensations like warmth/cold. I sometimes generate the symbols of the binary numbering system—a "0" means no, whereas a "1" means yes. As you gain proficiency with the yes-no, go-no-go, off-on, start-stop concept, you'll learn what form your answers take. Then you can ask more far-reaching types of questions.

Another way your inner self breaks through the conscious ego is by means of the hundreds of intuitive flashes or insights it sends you in the course of a day. Some of these intuitions are very strong and pass successfully through your conscious web of denial. These are neither malfunctions in your mental system nor hallucinations. They're a part of your "you" and are actually more real than your conscious thought, although you've probably trained yourself to believe the reverse.

The environment and the emotional setting affect intuition and the process of receiving answers. Most people believe that an open, loving, sharing atmosphere is conducive to the maximum use of your intuitions. Such an environment can be, but there are other settings that may also contribute to optimum intuitive insight. Frustration is one of these. When you're frustrated—meaning you're cut off like the frustrum of a cone from its main part—you're held back from something you want. This separation often creates a magnetic drawing-to process that heightens intuitive information. Consequently, you can help your subordinates increase their intuitive awareness by creating situations of frustration. Now: *This must be done carefully and without any thought of setting someone up to fail.* You do this so that they will succeed and grow. One way to produce frustration gently is to hold back on an explanation of how to do something; let the person work out the solution him- or herself. Be certain the person knows you're fully supportive of their efforts and are not casting them adrift without aid. It's like throwing someone into a pool of water and letting him or her discover how to swim while you're standing there on the edge of the pool (1) with a life preserver in your hands and (2) with a personal readiness to jump in yourself and save the person if necessary.

You get more in touch with your intuitions and hunches by doing it. You let these ideas come to you, judging neither the process that produces them nor the ideas themselves. Simply let them be; let it happen. Keep practicing. It will come.

Life Lessons

How managers respond to subordinates depends a lot on how they view life in general. Life is a lesson-learning experience. Just how we set it up is unique to each person. We have free will that we can choose to exercise or not exercise at any time. The future for each one of us is totally in our own hands. You, and everyone else around you, bring to your life exactly the experiences and the lessons you want and need.

If the future isn't set in concrete, it must consist of an infinite number of probable realities. Any path consists of numerous branches, and all the branches you don't follow represent "paths not taken." Because a path or a choice isn't followed—you chose your present job instead of another one that was available—doesn't mean that a part of you ceases to exist. You chose your current path, and it's important for you to realize that even if you don't consciously understand why you chose it, it's the best path for you. If you can accept that, you can consider the possibility that you and everyone else is perfect at this present moment. The over four billion human beings on this planet are precisely where they want to be *at this moment,* even if they don't choose to understand how or why.

We select experiences so that various life lessons are learned. However, sometimes we're only aware of the most superficial meanings. If you try something on your job and it doesn't work—like the introduction of a new computer—the deep and personal lesson isn't what went wrong with the computer. The real lesson has to do with the creation of physical concepts, the interaction between people, personal effectiveness, precognition, and a host of other factors. The individual and collective lesson is, in effect, designed by the participants long before the first conscious idea of the computer appears.

Because the Edsel is supposed to be the biggest single business blunder in history, let's look at the situation from a life-lesson point of view. Considering life lessons as they apply to probable realities, there were an infinite number of possible outcomes regarding the Edsel. One probable reality, the one the Ford executives planned, was that the automobile would become the hottest selling four-wheeled machine on the market. In another probable reality, the car took its place among the Ford, the Lincoln, and the Mercury as a solid performer in the Ford Motor Company product line. Now, I'm sure the question that creeps into your mind is this: If the Ford executives and managers create their own individual and collective realities, why didn't they create the Edsel as a successful project? The answer to that question is: They created the reality that *they wanted.* The inner lessons the event brought to each of them was more important than the external event. In a universal sense, the outcome of a project is neither good nor bad, neither right nor wrong; *it simply is.* The lessons learned are right for each person.

The life-lesson philosophy may be a bit hard for you to grasp if you establish your values from the physical world. You might believe success is important, but it's the lesson itself that's important, regardless of whether the outcome is viewed as success or failure. Too many people use the outcome rather than the lesson to generate future behavior. Early failures often are emphasized and become millstones when they really should be viewed as lessons and part of the self-renewing process.

All of your acquaintances and colleagues are engaged in this lesson-learning process. As a manager, you're a unique element in this experience and have a vital part in its course; don't believe what you do or anyone does is arbitrary and has no meaning. You chose to manage human beings, not assets, budgets, or methods, or even results the way you normally think of them. Your personal life-view manifests itself in and through both your consciousness and the part of you that seems to be unconscious or subconscious. It is your reality. Understand that each person has their unique reality that cannot, by definition, be your reality; their life lessons may not be yours. Respect and love these unique differences in others as you learn to love and respect your own.

Honesty: Still the Best Policy

Most people recognize that there's no such thing as absolute honesty. Honesty is a relative concept; but each of us knows what our personal honesty is. I'm not talking about honesty as the opposite of lying—telling a subordinate something that isn't true. I'm talking about openness. If you keep theories, ideas, feelings, and beliefs bottled up inside, they may create unpleasant conditions. If you harbor a certain belief about a subordinate (you believe Harry Jones is uninterested in his job and lazy), it's important for the two of you and your relationship that you tell Harry how you feel. Don't spend a lot of time fretting about your image or how Harry will accept your views. Deal openly and honestly with your feelings. People like to know where they stand. Initially, Harry may take your information and feel bad about it, but you already know Harry creates his own feelings and it's important for you to encourage him to communicate those emotions to you. It's possible you already sense his feelings on a telepathic level, but you may have conscious difficulty in translating that "broadcast." Once you start being open and honest, it quickly becomes second nature.

Some managers believe that honesty can be construed as some sort of brutality. "The truth always hurts." *Honesty* is honesty. *Brutality* is brutality. Your honesty is only the way you choose it to be; that's all it can be. If you communicate your honesty with love and a personal concern for others, it will come out that way.

Part of honesty is consistency. The last time I checked around, the biggest single complaint people had about their boss was that he or she is inconsistent. Say one thing, do another. Say one thing to top management, something else to the workers. Lecture the workers on tardiness and stroll in at 9:30. Treat Kathy differently from Fred. Stress adherence to company policy and then fail to follow it yourself when it suits you. All that stuff.

When you're inconsistent, you're lying. If you create dual personalities, you create more problems for yourself than solutions. Try to stay as close as you can to your true self. You know when you choose to ignore your true self—you can feel it.

Sense of Humor

Humor is a wonderful and readily available tonic with real therapeutic value to the human system, but it's very rare in many organizations. Most people take themselves and their work much too seriously. The next time you find yourself and your subordinate all caught up in a seriousness situation, give yourself the ten-year test. Ask yourself what difference all this will make ten years from now. I'll bet that it won't amount to anything at all, or at least it's not worth all the negative emotional fuss and bother you're investing in it.

I love to use humor in organizations even though some of it has fallen flat. On one occasion I was advising a manufacturing company on the construction of their first business plan. As a part of all this hectic activity, I gave a brief overview of the coming economic conditions to top management. I started my little talk with an introduction to economic indicators—those barometers of economy such as interest rates and unemployment levels that can foretell what is to come. I gave examples of some of these indicators and in a very serious way I mentioned that one economic indicator that was meaningful was the sale of duck feathers. "You know things will be great when even down is up." No laughter—just long faces and some nervous throat clearing.

That little pun was thought up in advance. Another was totally spontaneous. I was involved in a day-long meeting devoted to new products and pending corporate acquisitions. The new product receiving the most serious attention was a new brand of industrial adhesive—something to compete with what the Loc-tite organizations had done. At the same time, we were considering acquiring a manufacturing company whose main product line was industrial fasteners—screws, bolts, nuts of all kinds. One bright executive came up with an intuitive flash of brilliance; he suggested we simultaneously introduce the adhesive and buy the fastener company because we could mount a sales force selling two kinds of "fasteners"—one chemical and the other mechanical. To support his brainchild and break a relentless all-work-no-play day, I piped up that I already had the advertising slogan: "if you can't glue it, screw it!" Nothing.

Business does not have to be some kind of black-crepe-draped facility where people in symbolic sackcloth and ashes go around with long faces. You see it too often, though. The major objective of life is to enjoy the experiences you choose for yourself. It isn't a case of making the best of a bad situation; it's simply learning to love all facets of your being, to love others, to grow in wisdom, and to enjoy. Laugh at yourself when it's appropriate. Of course, you'll do some dumb things. We all do. Humor enables us to keep our perspective, to see the lessons rather than the limitations, red tape, and problems.

Encourage a light atmosphere. Let yourself and your people be natural, to yield to their natural humor. A soft answer turneth away wrath. Humor, like yawns, is contagious. Laughter often brings joy along with it. Spontaneity and the creativity that it spawns are born in joy. Your mental and physical health and that of your subordinates will improve.

Your emotions don't have to follow certain events. Just because a project, a study, or anything new doesn't turn out the way you and others want it to is no reason to spread gloom and foreboding. I'm not suggesting there aren't serious moments, but too many of the emotions I see in organizations are negative ones.

If you catch yourself getting distraught over something you don't want to, take a few minutes away by yourself. See the lighter, human side of things. Encourage spontaneity, joy, laughter; discourage rigidity, melancholy, discontent. Nothing has to be taken seriously, least of all yourself.

Agreements

The final aspect in our humane management of people has to do with expectations, specifically those bound by agreements of one form or another.

Life is a series of agreements, some stated, some not. Some known, some unknown. The simplest example of an unstated and often unknown agreement is the consent law accompanying a driver's license in most states. By applying for and accepting a license, you automatically consent to certain things such as the power of the state to take that license away for refusing to take a breathalyzer test or driving under the influence of alcohol. The consent law is usually something you read to pass your driver's test and then quickly forget.

A legal agreement is called a contract and has five elements—an offer, an acceptance, consideration (usually money), legality, and the competence of the parties to the contract (for example, an insane person or a minor cannot be held to a contract). For the most part, contracts are written documents, but they can be verbal.

Clean-cut known contracts, like a bill of sale for a car, usually cause little trouble between the parties. Oh, once in awhile someone tries to wriggle out of one clause or another, but by and large the execution and performance of most contracts and agreements goes on without overwhelming problems. It's within the realm of the unstated and especially unknown agreements that difficulties arise. Let's look at a typical situation.

Even before a person shows up for work on that first day, there exists in each of your minds some sort of contract or agreement. Each of you surrenders a legal right in terms of the employment contract that doesn't have to be written. As the employer, you give up the right to hire someone else for the same position; the new employee gives up the right to work for another organization during the same hours he or she works for you. That's the legal or stated part of things. When you accept this, you automatically agree to the unstated part of the agreement that has two parts. The first part concerns the policies of the organization; these may be formal and in writing or simply be in the minds of management. The second part of the unstated agreement includes all the

136

general beliefs, expectations, attitudes, conditions of work that are in the minds of employer and employee regarding the work.

When one party to an agreement discovers the "hidden agenda" of an agreement, it's normally pretty disturbing to them. I know I was stunned to discover the no-coffee policy that got me into so much trouble. The more a subordinate is aware of these unstated, unknown parts of an agreement *before* any fulfillment of the agreement is initiated, the better your relationship will be. When you and a subordinate discuss some project your subordinate is going to work on, you essentially enter an agreement. That agreement should be binding upon both of you, not from any kind of legal standpoint, but from the standpoint of your mutual integrity.

If you find you enter an agreement and something changes giving you the feelings you want out of the agreement or to change it, say so. Don't pretend the original conditions never existed—"Oh, that's not what we agreed to do at all." Either cancel the agreement with the open consent of the other party or establish a new one.

The most common reason people fail to live up to their part of a bargain is because something in the agreement isn't what they expected. Consequently, they want to get out of the entire agreement, often even creating behavior detracting from their overall performance. Were you ever promised a promotion that never came? Maybe it was only hinted at by your supervisor, but in your mind it was an inevitable truth. When it didn't occur, rather than simply acknowledging the reality that you didn't get what you wanted and moving on with the tasks at hand, did you begin conducting yourself in a way that demonstrated that your boss lied to you? Did you even consider quitting?

This is the process many people go through when unknown/ unstated agreements are broken. All this occurs because you believe your supervisor agreed to promote you when, in his mind, he did no such thing. When he fails to live up to his half of *your* bargain, you retaliate in negative behavioral changes. However, because he's unaware of this unstated/unknown agreement you've committed him to, can you blame him if he seems confused or unresponsive to your anger and hurt feelings? Or that he may choose to respond to you in a similar negative fashion?

When this situation arises, whether with a subordinate or superior, first *define* the nature of any agreement you perceive; then determine whether or not that agreement is mutually acceptable, needs to be changed, or should be discarded completely. What you definitely want to avoid is some midpoint nonsolution (bearing a grudge, quitting in a huff). This does nothing to solve the basic communication problem that created the situation in the first place.

Be careful about establishing a pattern where you fail to complete agreements. To me, the word *integrity* describes the quality of dependability—the assurance that when someone tells me they'll do something, there's a high probability they indeed will do it.

When we speak of an automated business world where timing is essential to productivity, integrity is important. You need to be able to depend on your subordinates; they need to be able to depend on you. In order for this mutually beneficial state to exist, you must be able to communicate. If unstated or unknown agreements exist, you and your subordinate must feel free to articulate them if either of you believe discrepancies arise.

A Manager's Creed

Many professions have creeds, oaths, canons, or codes of ethics they use to distill their philosophy into a readily available form. I've taken the material from these last two chapters and condensed it into a creed for managers. You may want to use this one, or you may want to write your own, either alone or with your people. The important thing is to understand how you feel about yourself, your workers, and your organization so you can respond consistently and without hesitation when problems arise. The process of computerization itself, as well as the number and types of problems resulting within a computerized workplace, are unique to the technology. You must be secure in your ability to deal with the human factors before you can successfully deal with the technological ones, not vice versa. Your people, not your equipment, should be the first, and perhaps even the only thing you're *sure* you can count on. Once you and your people agree on a management philosophy, whether or not everyone likes all aspects of it, you are well on your way to creating a work unit that can easily withstand all the equipment and procedural changes the computerized age has to offer. This is not to say that your philosophy will never change; in fact, it must change if it is to reflect the need and desire of every human being and organization to be creative and grow.

> *A Manager's Creed*
>
> You and I are in a relationship I value and want to keep, yet each of us is a separate person with his or her own unique needs and a desire to meet those needs. I will be accepting of your behavior when you are trying to meet your needs or when you are having problems meeting your needs.
>
> When you share your problems with me, I will listen acceptingly and understandingly in a way that will facilitate your finding your own solutions rather than depending totally upon mine. When you have a problem meeting your needs, I will encourage you to be open and honest about your feelings. At those times, I will listen and may modify my behavior if I believe the change you desire is possible. It is also important you realize

that just as you and I have a unique relationship, so I have a unique relationship with my supervisor.

When your behavior interferes with my meeting my own needs or the needs of the organization as I perceive them, I will share my problem with you and tell you how I feel, trusting you will respect my needs enough to listen and then modify your behavior if possible.

At those times when neither of us can modify his or her behavior to meet the needs of the other or the needs of the organization and we find that we have a conflict of needs in our relationship, let us commit ourselves to resolve each such conflict without ever resorting to the use of my power or yours to win at the expense of the other. I respect your needs and I respect my own and those of our organization; consequently, let us strive to search for solutions to our conflicts that will be acceptable to all. In this way, you can continue to develop as a person and so can I.

Our relationship can always be a healthy one because it will be mutually satisfying. Each of us can become what he or she is capable of being, and we can continue to relate to each other as we both grow with feelings of respect, with a deep and abiding love related to our mutual desire for each other to have what we want from our lives, in kinship for our common goals, and in lasting peace.

The Computer and Human Beings

11

You may love computers (a cyberphile); you may hate and fear them (a cyberphobe). You may believe the human race will meet its ultimate downfall at the hands of computers gone beserk, or you may see computers as mankind's savior. One thing is certain: Computers are here to stay and there will be more of them in our cars, pockets, briefcases, homes, and workplaces. Have we become dependent on them? If the "we" in that statement represents the industrialized, civilized nations of the world, the answer is "yes." If all the computers in the United States alone were tossed in the trash and we continued doing all the work manually, it would take at least one *billion* people (over four times the total United States population) to pick up the slack.

The relationship between computer and human being is symbiotic—each depends upon the other for existence. This statement might be a bit frightening at first, but the same can be said about the automobile, which was once so feared by a majority of the population that elaborate procedures were enacted in some locales to announce its approach. Some even called it the work of the devil. In like manner, many consider the computer the devil's work, and therefore something to be feared and hated. Because we all create our own realities, if someone fears a computer, they must fear a part or all of themselves. The existence and resolution of this fear falls squarely on the shoulders of the managers, supervisors, executives, and business owners responsible for the final decision to automate. If employees fear computerization, whatever the computer takes over must represent the limit of his or her ability as each employeee perceives it. Management *must* assure their staffs that their abilities far surpass the greatest computer that can ever be built. *That,* Mr. or Ms. manager, is one of your most important messages. Yes, we'll build more powerful information processors; we'll be able to mimic the human *brain*; but we can never emulate the human *mind.*

What Is a Computer—Really?

Is a computer alive? Suppose it is. Is that any greater threat to us than a cat, a leaf, a river? Let's go through some philosophical musings to dispel the greatest fear of all—that the computer has its own existence independent of the human race, and therefore is a threat to us.

What is the current definition of life? Cellular structure? Many people choose that one, so let's begin with the cell and break it down into its next smallest subdivision, molecules. Are molecules alive? Some experts say yes, some no. What about atoms? Subatomic particles? Where do we draw the line between the living and nonliving objects? Many metals have cellular structures and many modern physicists conclude that nuclear entities such as the electron behave as if they have a form of consciousness. Are metals and electrons alive or not?

If we describe life in terms of motion or lack of motion, are automobiles alive and rocks dead? Civilized human beings like to believe that all machines are things—dead, inanimate—and function only insomuch as they program them one way or another. Relative to this reality, any motion (life) present in any machine exists by virtue of human beings' creativity. This is a workable concept as long as we are able to deal with our creation on a one-to-one basis. When you drive a car or use a mixer, you rarely feel inadequate relative to the machinery. If nothing else, most people believe they can stop or even "kill" the car or mixer if necessary.

However, as we create machines of greater complexity, the number of parts often increases while the actual visible motion decreases or may not be apparent at all. Although we may acknowledge the existence of relatively strict criteria separating alive from dead, animate from inanimate, most of us intuitively recognize their total arbitrariness; then everything becomes complicated. If we look at the human body as it sleeps and apply our criterion of motion, is it dead or alive? As soon as we answer "alive," motion can no longer be a valid test. If we decide upon vibratory motion as our criterion for life, we can use the heartbeat or breathing to indicate life, and that definition holds for both sleeping and wakened persons. Humans are pleased with this definition for they are historically frightened that they might die during their sleep. Many of us grew up learning the child's prayer that starts "Now I lay me down to sleep," and ends "I pray the Lord my soul to take." With our new definition of vibratory motion—in/out, contraction/relaxation—rather than linear motion defining life, we free ourselves of this ancient fear.

Unfortunately, this new definition also creates problems. For although we may now sleep in peace and embrace members of the plant kingdom as brothers and sisters, we must also consider the vibratory motion of such unnatural states as machines—particularly large machines that produce barely audible or sensed vibrations like ourselves. Cyberphobia is not a new disease. Humans have been afraid of machines in one way or another since time and humans began together. What many in this position fail to realize is that they're up against their own definition of life; if it's limited and the machine exceeds their definition of themselves, it's conceivable that the machine could overpower them. What Dr. Frankenstein didn't come to grips with is the fact that no creator can create something greater than him- or herself.

If I suspend you by a rope over the side of an oceangoing vessel proceeding at full speed, or from the doorway of a plane at several thousand feet, very few would consider your fear a neurosis or an unfounded phobia. Had you presided over the creation of either that ocean and vessel or the plane and the sky, you would probably have few if any fears at all. In the past, the evolution of machinery has been to mechanize those physical acts with which we were familiar. Humans progressed from walking to horseback to bicycles to cars. Automatic washers and sewing machines took common human physical *acts* and made them more efficient. Production machines and conveyor belts did the same. But always it was a case of taking something quite common, quite physical, and increasing its rate or otherwise increasing its efficiency. Thus we may say that relative to the great majority of machines that surround them, most people feel they participated in and therefore understand their evolution. Just as the developing embryo goes through phases consistent with the peculiarities of *all* species, so the man who runs the crane has intuitive memories of the first men and his own childhood attempts to use lever, pulley, and wheel to expand his abilities.

However, computers ask us to take a major leap in two different directions simultaneously. For the first time in history, a machine has been created whose innermost workings are primarily intuitive to the vast majority of the population. Few people understand where the computer "came from," even though they now appear everywhere. Consequently, the majority of the population view a computer as a *fait accompli* of great potential that is troublesome because its most common human analogy is "This machine is like my mind." In essence, computers function as manifestations of another reality, that of the mind; and if individuals aren't comfortable with, or are threatened by, such a concept, they're invariably comfortable with and threatened by computers.

Of the handful of people privy to the real creation of the computer, few seem willing or able to share its true nature with others. They balk at human analogies, whereas those outside this inner circle view a machine whose evolution is not clear to them in strongly human terms. If you say to someone, "The computer will do your addition and subtraction for you," the intutive response is that the computer replaces pencil and paper in the same way the typewriter did. But it doesn't; it replaces the mind. "It replaces me." That's a very logical deduction—which is why responses based on logic are so ineffective.

Even when the computer's creators try to reassure us by referring to the computer's origins in the minds of men, it seems such a magical, inner circle they speak of and to, not unlike the high priests of old entrenched in their inaccessible temples. And when they do choose to speak, they speak a language few understand. In short, the computer is the culmination of mankind's desire to create humans' minds in mass form, to remove the emotion (bias) from a fabric whose bias is indicative of its elasticity and creativity. For those who don't want to relinquish this part of the self, the computer is most threatening. For those who see themselves as too rigid in their thinking already, the computer is also threatening. Thus, the computer as an intuitive model mind threatens the entire continuum of human mentality. For just as the individual who is terrified of self-flights into fantasy often fears both planes and heights, so those who fear the workings of their own mind will fear computers.

Let's briefly summarize: First, when we define imperceptible motion as life, certain machines invariably fit that definition. Suddenly the computer becomes potentially alive. Second, mechanical evolution traditionally follows a path of close approximation; a human *act* was mechanically enhanced in a logical progression. Even though we may say machines such as automatic pilots replace humans, the strong evolution and logical progression leading to their creation makes them dead machines. Third, the creation of the computer is the manifestation of the desire of a large segment of mankind to understand and communicate more easily between "here" (the body) and "there" (the mind). Technologically, the computer is the most exquisite example of mass "here"; in order to understand it here, one needs an equivalent amount of awareness "there." No other machine or mass creation has ever required so much from the human body, mind, and spirit. To be sure, one can say, "It's only a keyboard or a calculator," and so that's all it is to those people. That's like looking at a pack of seeds and saying, "These are only seeds. It's all that they can be."

If, on the other hand, you view the computer as the mechanical manifestation of a unique relationship (as the computer designer or programmer views the device as an extension of his or her own creativity), the results are quite different. If one isn't committed to the relationship in terms of its advantages to one's own creativity (that is, self-wisdom and self-love), then such relationships, be they with machines, people, animals, or plants, can only manifest themselves to the limit that each individual is willing to invest.

The result is obvious: garbage in, garbage out; fear in, fear out; hesitation in, hesitation out; minimal commitment in, minimal commitment out.

Some people may see this book as a work on computers, others as a management handbook, and still others may call it philosophy. It's all three. What I want to give you is an awareness that the information processor is not just another kind of a machine. The computer should not be relegated to the category of mundane hardware that we must endure; neither should it be held in awe or fear. Your approach to the management of human beings must change in response to the changes in technology; if it doesn't, the computer cannot be seen as positive and beneficial to yourself, your subordinates, and your organization.

We hear that a new age is about to dawn, an age not only of personal enlightenment but also a new age of technology. This technology is neither the slave of mankind nor its master; it is an equal partner in our future development and worthy of our human respect and consideration.

Index